PENGUIN BOOKS

THE VISIBLE INVISIBLES: STORIES OF MIGRANT WORKERS IN ASIA

Shivaji Das is the author of four critically acclaimed travel, art and business books. He was the first prize winner for *Time* Magazine's Sub-Continental Drift Essay contest and shortlisted for Fair Australia Prize for Short Stories.

Shivaji has been actively involved in migrant issues and is the conceptualizer and organizer for the acclaimed Migrant Worker and Refugee Poetry Contests in Singapore, Malaysia and Kenya and is the founder and director of the Global Migrant Festival.

Shivaji's work and his interviews have been featured on BBC, CNBC, The Economist, Travel Radio Australia, Around the World TV, etc. Shivaji's writings have been published in magazines such as *TIME*, *South China Morning Post*, *Think China*, *Asian Geographic*, *Jakarta Post*, *Conscious* Magazine, *PanaJournal*, *Freethinker*, etc.

Shivaji Das was born and brought up in the north-eastern province of Assam in India. Shivaji is a graduate from IIT Delhi and has an MBA from IIM Calcutta. He works as the Managing Director-APAC for Frost & Sullivan, a research and consulting company. Shivaji is currently a Singapore citizen.

Yolanda Yu is a multi-time winner of the Golden Point Award. Her book *Neighbor's Luck*, a collection of short stories was shortlisted for the Singapore Literature Award 2020. Yolanda's work has been featured on *LianHe ZaoBao*, *Cha* Journal, *New York Times Travel*, *Zuopin* Magazine, and *Guangxi Literature* Magazine. Her story 'The Twelfth Man' has been adapted for a film, while her story 'The Missing Clock' is a recommended read for O-Level students by Singapore's Ministry of Education, collected in the anthology *How We Live Now*.

Yolanda is a co-organizer of the Singapore Migrant Worker Poetry Contest and Global Migrant Festival, also an event host and coordinator for outreach for the Chinese migrant worker community.

Born in North-Eastern China, Yolanda came to Singapore on scholarship in 1998 and has been living there since then. She holds a Computer Science degree from the National University of Singapore and an MBA from INSEAD Business School. After her twenty years of corporate career, Yolanda is now an Executive Coach for career and leadership development.

ADVANCE PRAISE FOR *THE VISIBLE INVISIBLES:*
STORIES OF MIGRANT WORKERS IN ASIA

Shivaji and Yolanda have a special talent for extracting and distilling information from people that many of their readers will never meet, struggling in circumstances that many will never experience. These are indeed depressing stories, but also very human and compelling, as we are introduced to their families, their aspirations, and their sacrifices, sometimes with optimism, and sometimes with resignation and despair. May the stories in this book remind us of the brilliance and sanctity in every person. May this book enable us to see how the labour of many individuals makes possible the growth and prosperity of wealthy societies, and that our tolerance of these inequalities betrays the idea of what economic success should guarantee.

—Debbie Fordyce, activist for migrant workers,
President, TWC2 Singapore

Migrant workers often emigrate to escape from the harsh reality and discrimination brought about by unfair social distribution, as well as the exploitation and alienation brought about by capital and power. While they come to a foreign land with a lot of hope, they often struggle between survival and life. We should listen to the voices of the migrant workers. They deserve the world's attention and contemplation. In this outstanding work, the authors capture these voices with sympathy and compassion, clearly demonstrating their plight and suffering without being patronizing.

—Zheng Xiaoqiong, noted poet and
erstwhile migrant worker

Migrants, who do essential work that makes modern life possible, are not so much invisible as they are unheard of. A cook in a restaurant kitchen, a nanny pushing a pram in a park, or a carpenter on a swaying scaffold, are all visible. But the way they see their own lives is terra incognita to the people who live around them. Shivaji Das and Yolanda Yu hear and collect their voices to present an incredible variety of migrants' stories in *The Visible Invisibles*. These are not predictable stereotypes, but colourful and moving accounts of life experienced by those right next to us. If you think you know or can predict how migrants feel about their lives, this book makes you realize that you don't. Check out this collection and laugh and cry at what you find.

—David Bacon, noted photojournalist, author,
political activist, and union organizer, USA

Drenched with sweat, on the building site,
shops, restaurants, plantations and factories,
is our struggle and real contribution to development.
I and thousands of my brothers want to live like you
Look at us like fellow human beings of God

Beneath this country's sky . . .
I try to enquote the spread of prosperity

I am your brother, permit me . . .

Translation of an excerpt from the poem *Di Bawah Langit Negeri Ini* (Beneath This Country's Sky) by Figo Kurniawan, former migrant worker from Indonesia to Malaysia.

* * *

Ours is not a foreign life
Our lives are foreign to us.

From the poem, 'The Calculations of Migrant Life', by N Rengarajan, former migrant worker from India to Singapore, translated from the Tamil by Krishna Udayasankar and Gopika Jadeja.

* * *

I know not how to protect a voiceless life
This nameless and sexless life, this life of contract . . .

From the poem, 'Life', by Zheng Xiaoqiong, former domestic migrant worker in China, poet and editor, translated from the Chinese by Zhou Xiaojing.

The Visible Invisibles: Stories of Migrant Workers in Asia

Shivaji Das and Yolanda Yu

PENGUIN BOOKS

An imprint of Penguin Random House

PENGUIN BOOKS

USA | Canada | UK | Ireland | Australia
New Zealand | India | South Africa | China | Southeast Asia

Penguin Books is part of the Penguin Random House group of companies
whose addresses can be found at global.penguinrandomhouse.com

Published by Penguin Random House SEA Pte Ltd
9, Changi South Street 3, Level 08-01,
Singapore 486361

First published in Penguin Books by Penguin Random House SEA 2022

ISBN 9789815017786

Typeset in Garamond by MAP Systems, Bangalore, India

www.penguin.sg

Contents

Introduction

After the finals of Singapore's first Migrant Worker Poetry Competition in 2014, many from the audience—mostly comprised of locals—made a common patronizing comment, 'Wow, migrant workers are humans too, just like us'. The migrant workers, on their part, were visibly eager to take selfies with any willing locals in the audience, pictures that they then shared widely on social media. These two separate but related reactions made us wonder: how big was the gap in understanding between locals and low-wage migrant workers?[1] Why are there so few avenues—other than across supermarket tills—for interaction between the two categories? Why do we know so little about this highly visible group of people who are building our houses and roads or taking care of our children and elders? Does this apathy in any way affect the policies designed for them, a group of people who typically stand out because of their physical appearance, work attire, or manner of speech? So what if we were to know about their childhood? What if we knew more about the circumstances that made them migrate? What if we knew about their love stories, their grudges, their hopes, aspirations, and heartbreaks? Could greater understanding lead to more humane policies and structural changes?

---

[1] Different jurisdictions have different definitions for low-wage migrant workers: by salary, path to residency, etc. We have largely followed the corresponding work permit guidelines in relevant jurisdictions.

Migration of labour is one of the most defining characteristics of our world today. Over a billion people are living in a place where they were not born. Among them, around 281 million[2] are international migrants while the rest are domestic (internal) migrants. A vast majority of migrants happen to be migrant workers, of the lower-wage category, those tempted or forced to move as a result of economic stagnation, political instability, identity-based discrimination, or climate change. In contrast to higher-income migrants who often have a path to citizenship in their host country and the economic wherewithal to fight for their rights or move to a more convenient location; the low-wage migrant workers, whether international or domestic, face crippling challenges such as exorbitant agent fees, informal and unenforceable nature of contracts, poor living conditions, hostility from locals, and denial of any political agency.

This collection—focusing solely on the life journeys of low-wage migrant workers as narrated by them in their own words—hopes to foster greater understanding between locals and migrants. Our underlying belief behind this effort is that with understanding comes political agency, and with political agency, come positive structural changes.

For the purpose of this book, we interviewed forty-five current and former migrant workers whose experiences span across various jobs: construction, marine, domestic services, aged care, mining, manufacturing, plantation work, security services, retail, mixed day-labour, and sexual services. We sought biographical accounts of both domestic and international migrant workers; the featured men and women coming from the major sources of migrant labour in Asia: Bangladesh, China, India, Indonesia, Myanmar, Nepal, Sri Lanka, and the Philippines.

In our conversations, we asked about childhood experiences, factors influencing the decision to migrate, work experiences, as well as relationships with employers, other workers and the wider society. We explored themes of power imbalances, love, language, friendship,

---

[2] Source: World Migration Report 2020, by International Organization for Migration (IOM)

alienation, family dynamics, response to cultural contrasts, race relations, digital inequality, social liberties, migration-induced change in mindset, etc. We were interested in both the physical and the emotional landscape. Also while the situation of low-wage migrant workers is all too often narrated by third parties—an NGO, an academician, or a journalist—the perspectives provided here are from the 'I' rather than the 'they'.

The life-stories in this book span universal themes of longing, love, ambition, loss and the spirit of adventure among others. Zhou Hongxing picks up a discarded teddy bear lying by the trash bin as a gift for his daughter. Durga Balan mourns the death of his best friend in an industrial accident. Ah Linn Eain, a fatherless girl also rejected by her own mother, becomes a migrant worker to support her orphaned niece while dreaming of building an orphanage back home. Figo Kurniawan recounts his days spent in the wild, hiding from the police looking for undocumented workers. Ataur Rahman tries to rebuild his life with a reconstructed 'alien' face after suffering severe burns at work. Faced with COVID-19 restrictions, Mai and Aomsin scramble to cope with the complete loss of customers for their sex-work while Vijaykanth, stressed from lockdown, finds solace playing with toys in a toy store. Chen Nian Xi looks at his X-ray scan and in it, sees a catalogue of his work injuries from his sixteen years of being a miner. A.K. Zilani shares how the anonymity of migration facilitated his evolution as a freethinker with progressive ideals. Lovely Comavig, runs away from her husband who's set out to kill her, and finds love in her host city. Sagar struggles to catch-up with the never ending demands of his family back home. Lalita Vadia, freed from traffickers posing as employment agents, supports other migrant workers now. Zhou BoTong and Dilip both gamble frequently, hoping to strike it big one day. Wiwi, Deni, and Sugi share tips for dating in a foreign land.

Striking similarities appear across borders and jurisdictions with respect to the issues and challenges faced by low-wage migrant workers. But while most complain of discrimination from locals, the featured individuals also demonstrate strong prejudices against fellow migrant workers from other races.

Migrant workers, devoid of any political representation, often find themselves fighting a giant system that is unfavourable to them. But workers such as Rajendra, Mai and Aomsin—through their own formal and informal networks such as unions, collectives, etc.—are demonstrating a certain ability to fight for their rights. Nonetheless, the stories here make it apparent how policies and their consistent enforcement remain critical for any improvement in their situation.

The individual stories have been largely presented as told by the migrant workers themselves, with minor edits for clarity, consistency and flow. For conversations conducted in languages other than English, we have translated them ourselves, at times aided by interpreters. We have, however, refrained from sharing any narrative from our own interpretations; all views presented in this book are only those of the featured migrant workers. For those worried about revealing their identities, we have used pseudonyms or aliases, often chosen by the concerned individual.

Overall, this collection presents an archive of human miseries: discrimination, injustice, exploitation, alienation and social immobility. But by repeatedly demonstrating a certain pride in their work, resilience amidst adversity, a strong feeling of solidarity for all workers, and an all-conquering sense of hope and determination to uplift an entire generation and beyond, the featured life-stories of migrant workers firmly endorse the reaffirming qualities of human life.

It was our privilege and honour to record these life-journeys.

Yolanda Yu and Shivaji Das
February 2022, Singapore

Part I

Is becoming a migrant worker a matter of choice, or a lack thereof? How much do circumstances beyond one's control, the family and society someone was born into or the timing of birth, play a part? Some feel as if the choice was already made for them while some attempt for conciliation with 'destiny'. Some question 'why me?'

In this section, the featured migrant workers—Christian E. Comingking (The Philippines), Ah Linn Eain, Lantern (Myanmar), and Chen Nian Xi (China)—dwell on these issues and more as they narrate their life stories.

Why is Everyone Else So Complete?

Christian E. Comingking (The Philippines),
thirty-one years old, Caregiver, worked in Kuwait,
currently working in Malaysia

I was born the year after the big typhoon season of 1990 when flash floods destroyed much of Leyte, my province.

My father was a fisherman and my mom is a housewife. We are seven siblings, four brothers and three sisters. I am number five. Actually, we were fourteen siblings but the others died.

My house is by the seaside. During high tide, the water comes right underneath. My best memories from my childhood are the times my father took me to the sea. He would wake me up at 5 a.m. and say, 'Come, son. Let's go and get our crabs.' We made the cages out of bamboo and put marinated fish inside as bait. Then after a few weeks, we pulled up the cages and there would be many crabs inside. I also loved those times when he took me to the jungle. He would call, 'Come, son. Let's go and get some firewood.' It was so good to have such nice bonding with my father.

My dearest father died when I was only twelve years old. You know what? That time I had this opportunity to study in a really good private institution, the Sisters of Mary School, Boystown complex. It's a big school in Cebu, run by the Catholics. I could study there for free, on a scholarship. My parents had told me that it was difficult for them to send me to high school because my elder siblings were going to college and my father was struggling to pay my fees. Luckily, I got this scholarship. It was a big blessing. But during my first year there, my father caught tuberculosis. That time I didn't know anything about my father's suffering. Let me tell you a really strange incident—you wouldn't believe me. But one night, when I was sleeping in the school dormitory, I had a strange dream. I saw my father inside a coffin. I saw our house. Why were there so many people inside? Suddenly my father got up from the coffin. He wanted to touch my hands and legs. I woke up. I was shaking. Everyone around my bunk bed woke up from my screams. They asked what happened, why are you shouting for help? The next morning, our sister-in-charge called me and asked me a lot of questions about my father, his occupation, and our family. I got triggered. I shouted, 'Okay, sister. I already know my father has died. He visited in my dreams. I already know.' Sister Raya was shocked. There were tears in her eyes. She asked me if I wanted to go back home—the school could pay for my trip—but warned me that my family might not send me back to study. I didn't want to give up my four-year scholarship. I was not being selfish but I thought that now that my father is dead, they might really ask me to start working. So I just told Sister Raya that, 'Sister, I'm willing to continue this opportunity because no one will send me to school again. My relatives also are in same situation as me. I better stay here as long as I have to. I have the courage to continue and my father will be my inspiration.' So I didn't go back. I couldn't see my father for the last time. That was the darkest day in my life.

Those days, we were not using phones. Once you were inside the complex, there was absolutely no communication with the outside world. In one year, I would receive only one visitor. When my aunt visited me, she told me that my mother had had a nervous breakdown after my father's death. She was having severe depression. When I finally went home during the school break, I saw my mother acting like a child. She walked naked. She was violent. Our family had tied her with a chain. I was so shocked. That day I cried a lot.

My eldest brother and sister dropped out of college and started working as salespeople in shops. They gave up their dreams to buy clothes and rice for the rest of us. But the money was not enough. We couldn't eat three times a day. We had to go to the Captain of our *barangay*[3] and ask, can we have some sardines or noodles, just to ease our hunger. When I saw that situation, I decided to start working. I wanted to lift up our family situation. I was not aiming very high; I just didn't want ourselves to remain at such a low level. I wanted to make a change.

My first job was at my uncle's vegetable stall. But I didn't like being dependent on relatives. So I found work in a hospital, as an office clerk. I worked in the morning and then studied at night. I took many short courses—all technical vocational education ones—like general metals technology, then computer, then electro-mechanical, industrial sewing, housekeeping, housekeeping in situ, caregiving in situ. But these were never in a formal college.

In December 2017, I got my chance. I got a job in Kuwait, as a caregiver for a sick person at home. I was so lucky. I didn't have to pay any agent. I was a member of a Facebook group where there were job postings for caregivers. I saw this listing there. I was so lucky. The employer was a very nice person. He didn't know me but still trusted me completely. We just chatted and I got hired. He is also a Christian, same like me, and from the same church.

When I came to Kuwait, I was really so excited. It was my dream job. It was my first time overseas. My expectations were very high, that I will spend my life nicely, that the place will be nice, the food will be nice. But when I got there, it was like the opposite. My happiness and excitement lasted only six months. I enjoyed my work but I felt so lonely, depressed, and homesick. Sometimes I cried alone. My family never contacted me. They never asked, 'How are you? Did you eat? How's the work?' My friends there were lucky because their families always contacted them. But it was always me who was telling my family that I was okay, without them asking. The whole day, I could only

---

[3] Neighbourhood administrative unit in the Philippines

talk to my boss, in basic Arabic, and to the other caregiver, an Indian man who was like a nice uncle to me. We were not allowed to talk to any of the female members in the house because it was like haram[4] to them. In this new environment, it was like I could only see out from the windows; the cars, the park, the people, but I couldn't talk to anyone. I was so thirsty for speaking my native language. Only on holidays, I could go out, to the supermarket, mall, or to the church. My church friends helped me and encouraged me a lot. But I would still remain empty, sad, homesick and lonely. Yeah, but I still struggled and continued for two years, and then I couldn't continue anymore.

But I had to help my family. So I came to Malaysia, in September 2019. I spent around 7,000 ringgit—on agent, on flights, and other expenses—just to come here. I work in a care home where I look after old people, managing their daily routine like grooming, showering. I am happier here because here I have a lot of teammates, from the Philippines, from India. There are twenty of us. I am good friends with them. The ambience is same same like Philippines and I am able to talk in my native language. There are even people from the Visayas so I can speak my dialect too. In Kuwait, I had to learn Arabic but here we're not learning any Bahasa Melayu—only *makan, tidur, tandas*[5]—because we can always manage using English.

I am hired as a caregiver but we are actually doing a lot more like housekeeping, laundry, cooking. It's the opposite of what I was expecting. It is totally different from the contract. Each one of us is supposed to take care of only two residents but we actually care for six to eight, 24/7. Here I get so many night shifts. When I came here, they also sent me to the kitchen because I also got this talent of cooking. I had to cook for all forty people, staff and residents every day. The woks and casseroles are so heavy. Then we also have to constantly lift and move the residents, from wheelchairs to various places. The residents are so big, like huge size, like extra-large. They also slap us, beat us, punch us, spit at us, kick us. But that is part of our job.

---

[4] An act that is forbidden in Islam
[5] Words in Bahasa Malayu: makan (eat), tidur (sleep), tandas (toilet)

We know they have mental conditions like dementia so it is our duty to bear with that. That is not a problem. That is our passion. So I am still happy here.

But soon I got hernia from all this lifting of the residents and the kitchenware. I kept this to myself for the first three months. I was worried that the company would send me back. It was very painful. These were some of my darkest days. Finally, I couldn't take it.

When I told the management about my hernia, they asked me to go back to the Philippines because they didn't want to shoulder my expenses. 'You shouldn't abuse the insurance,' they said even though it was a work injury. I said, 'Okay, but boss, please promise me that you will take me back after my surgery. I need this job for my family, because I have a big table to feed.'

I paid for my own ticket and went back. I found a government hospital in the Philippines where they did my surgery for free. After the surgery, I was very delicate. Yet I came back to Malaysia just before the COVID lockdown, otherwise I would have been stuck. I was so lucky. At work, I began doing all the heavy lifting again. Luckily the surgery was good and I haven't had any problems for the last two years.

Okay, actually let me open up to you and share something I haven't told others. The workload here is stressful. That is still manageable. But there is a lot of racism, especially from this one lady who is my manager. She is always so rude with us Filipinos while she is nice with employees from other races. Like when we are eating, she will come and switch off the lights and fans saying it is time to work or that we should move to some other table. I was shocked. It's like no manners really. Then the management keeps following us everywhere like a CCTV, picking faults with everything. 'Why are you washing the plates so early? Did you take care of your residents there? Did you clean the area? Did you do your paperwork?' So recently, I burst into anger and I had a big fight with the management because they were treating Filipinos like so low and uneducated, that's why I became their voice when I talked to management. I was just so angry that day. But I still spoke respectfully. I told the boss that I wanted changes in the management. I told her that we were struggling, not because of the work but because the management was not treating us nicely, that the issues were getting toxic. People were abusing their power, torturing us mentally, emotionally. I was not scared when I said all this because I knew that the boss liked my work. Since then, things have been better.

All this is stressful. So sometimes, when I have free time, I go swimming or go for walks. I also bought seeds online and I planted them in our hostel garden. I have squash, pumpkin, kang kong, celery, and eggplant. I take care of them.

I was planning to go back home last September; I was actually thinking of going back for good. I want to start a tilapia fish plant. I want to study in a formal college. But I realized that I had savings of only 4,000 ringgit. As per my contract, the company had been deducting 300 ringgit from our salary every month as employment expenses, that deduction just got over. I asked God, 'Am I doing the right thing, Lord? Lord, help me, guide me.' Then with his help, I made this final decision to stay because it's not the appropriate time yet. My family still needs me to work in Malaysia. I am like a bird in a cage, like no freedom because I got this burden to send money back to the Philippines. But I am happy now. Our family situation is much better. My mother's mental situation has recovered. My eldest brother and eldest sister are supporting my family. So nowadays, I'm sending back a smaller amount of money. I even have some left for my necessities. Our salary here is only 1,800 ringgit every month. Out of that, I am sending 500 to my mother for her pocket money and another 500 for the instalment for my investment in land, a small lot in my village. With the remaining 800, I can buy my food and necessities and have some small savings.

Sure, I doubted God a lot. Every time I saw complete families, like the mother and father walking while holding hands of their children, I really confronted God. I said, 'God why, why are you like this to me? Why are you like this to my family? Why did you do this to us? Like why did you take my father so early? Why am I so poor?' Every time I saw children wearing white uniforms, like going to nursing school or medicine school, I would be so jealous. I would be crying.

Why are all these children able to go to school without any problems? Why can everyone else be complete? Because you know what? My father's plan was to make us all teachers. He wanted all of us siblings to take education courses. But that never happened. Really. That's why I confronted God. That's why I doubted God. Then slowly, I thought that all that happens is with a purpose. Maybe God took away my father so early just to make us independent, so we can make our own decisions in life. Other children are abusing their privilege, like they are just not doing good in school and just wasting their parent's money. You know in the Philippines, they say the men are very lazy and always gambling or drinking but it has been the opposite for me because I was so independent from early on. I never followed my relatives who are just lazy drunkards, just sitting all day, doing nothing. Then slowly, slowly, slowly, slowly, I think, like, I accept God. Also, being a Christian is a great help for me because all my church colleagues are always encouraging me. They encourage me to continue, to just go on with life.

I got this big dream of studying in a formal college but it was not affordable. In my first job, I saw the doctors and I want to become like them. That's the second reason why I work overseas because I want to save enough so I can study and become a doctor. But now, it's like a 360 degree change. I have set aside everything to just focus on the family. So maybe now it's not the exact time but I'm still not losing hope. If I'm stable soon, I will pursue my dream. We must not lose hope. There is still a brighter future ahead of us. We must carry on with life.

Twice, I Attempted Suicide

*Ah Linn Eain, Lantern (name changed), (Myanmar),
Thirty-eight years old, Cleaner in Singapore*

I was born in a *kampong*[6] far from Yangon. My father had no proper job. He often fought with my mother. He also had another woman in our kampong. My mother had a tough life and had to beg her sister-in-law for money. When I was six, my mother ran away with another man.

My five elder brothers were already grown up by then. They had already left home. My father was always drunk, he didn't care for me at all. I was sent to live with my aunt. My aunt's family was poor and didn't have enough for themselves. They saw me as 'bad luck'. My grandfather hated me and beat me. Neighbours teased me by asking if I missed my mother, and insulted me saying I'd become a bad woman like her. I was lonely and sad. I cried a lot.

When I was fourteen, my father passed away. I couldn't focus on my studies. I missed my mother too much. I tried to commit suicide by eating many sleeping pills. My cousin took me to the hospital; I was saved.

My aunt saw my unhappiness and asked me to look for my mother in Yangon. By then, my mother had split with the other man. But she refused to take me in.

---

[6] Village

My auntie called me back. I tried to commit suicide again, this time by cutting my wrist. They sent me to the hospital and again I was saved. But even today, the scar on my wrist remains deep and long. Everyone can see it. Yet finally, I realized that I shouldn't miss my mother any more. There was no point.

After this incident, I focused on my studies. A teacher helped me a lot and I managed to pass O-Level despite many unlucky things—a dog had bitten me and for two months I was too sick to even stand. The day the results came out, I ran out of the house, forgetting to even wear my shoes. I was the happiest person on earth.

My auntie passed away soon thereafter. I started working to support my part-time studies; my cousins helped me as well. I had a dream to graduate from a university. I wanted to earn a lot of money.

Around then, one of my elder brothers and his wife died in an accident, leaving behind their three-year-old daughter. Looking at the little orphaned girl, I felt so sad; she was just like me. I wanted to take care of her by paying for all her expenses. So I stopped my studies and took up whatever random jobs I could get, being a street seller, construction worker, nanny, receptionist . . . Eventually, I came to Singapore to work as a domestic worker.

My first employer was a fish seller in a wet market. He talked very loudly in Hokkien. I couldn't understand him and was always scared thinking he was scolding me. The family ate only porridge every day, but I was used to eating rice in Myanmar. I couldn't eat properly and was always hungry. I asked my agency to change employer. The agency refused to help till I threatened to run away without paying off my debt, amounting to eight months of my salary.

The second employer was much better. But the problem there though was their elder daughter. She was very naughty and bullied me a lot. She always blamed her wrongdoings on me. Her parents had a rule of not allowing strangers in the house. She brought friends home and covered up all the CCTVs, later blaming me for this. The parents became angry with me and after two years terminated my contract.

I changed employers many times, sometimes working as a domestic worker, sometimes as a caregiver. Each place had its own problem.

When I worked in elderly care, some old people were very difficult and yet I couldn't get angry . . . it would show up in the CCTV. So I left many jobs, each time going back to Myanmar and then coming back to Singapore with a new employer.

Now I work in Singapore as a cleaner. I have been doing this for eight years. I am still liking it. The big boss likes me. I can speak English with Singaporeans, so my customers also like me. I make more money as a cleaner than as a domestic worker. They pay me around 1,300 Singapore dollars a month, without any transportation or accommodation. Unlike a domestic worker who works till late at night, I'm free after 6 p.m. My mind is free and I have no pressure. I have many friends to hang out with. I can invite them to my own rented house and cook for them. It's just that my work is a bit tiring. Some of the houses I have to clean are so dirty; they haven't been cleaned for a long time.

But it's not easy being a foreign worker—our supervisors bully and scold us a lot. They are arrogant. They think foreign workers are stupid and illiterate. Once, I was cleaning a house and my Singaporean supervisor left after giving me instructions. The Ma'am (customer) was fussy and kept asking me to clean some areas again and again. The Ma'am then gifted me ten dollars, saying I did a good job, and that she'd call me if she had cleaning jobs again. But later my supervisor scolded me badly saying I took too long to finish too little work. I explained that it was because of the customer's requirements. The supervisor shouted at me, 'You so *Yaya*[7]. If you don't want to do work then just go home!' I cried hearing this.

I want to leave this company by the end of this year. Other companies pay more than here. But my big boss doesn't let me leave.

On Sundays, many Myanmar people, men and women, gather around City Hall to enjoy their off-day. These men and women first connect through Facebook and WhatsApp groups. The men work in construction, restaurants and shipyards. Sometimes the higher-income engineers also come. The girls are domestic workers or they work in restaurants or nursing homes. Some girls dress up sexy sexy . . . they

---

[7] Arrogant

find boyfriends, drink beer, dance together, all so messy. Alone in a foreign country, one can easily become a bad girl, start flirting around or make money through sex. I don't join them and I don't go there. I'm concerned of COVID-19, but more importantly, I don't want to be like them.

I did have a boyfriend here when I came the first time. He was not understanding at all—kept calling me during my work hours and got angry when I didn't pick up. I stopped the relationship and never wanted one since then. He's married now. Most people here become boyfriend and girlfriend just for fun. They break up when one of them goes back to their home country. 70 per cent of the men have family back home and are not serious with relationships here. I don't want all these.

I have strong memories of my first love. I met him when I was seventeen. We were classmates. He always supported, protected and cared for me. I didn't mind that he was also from a poor family. But I was scared of becoming like my mum: get married, have children, but then have no money to take care of the children . . . I wanted to be able to support myself. So, when he proposed, I said, 'Wait, wait, let me make money first. You make money and I also make money.' He waited. Ten years later, when I was twenty-seven, he asked again, and again I said, 'Wait . . .'. He didn't wait any longer. He married another woman. This makes me very sad.

Now he works in a government job and makes very little money. I have money and I'm happy being alone. I think I made the right decision. I don't want to have my own family. I have bought a house on instalment in Yangon which makes me happy enough. We met once as friends in Myanmar and he asked me whether I'd say yes if he proposed again. I told him I wouldn't because he had a family with children and I'd never break any family. I feel so sad for the children of broken families. My auntie took care of me but still I felt like an orphan. I'll never recover from that feeling.

I have been reading Buddhist scriptures since I was a teenager; they have helped me through difficult times. My teacher says that all my trouble was karma from bad deeds in past life. Now that I am growing old, I must do good for my next life. I live by the disciplines in the scriptures, I go to temple, meditate, help those who are suffering, and fight for those who are being bullied.

I haven't gone back home for three years now due to COVID-19. Things have been difficult in Myanmar. Everyone is scared. No one knows about the future. I lost a brother and a sister-in-law to COVID. My other brother has been doing random jobs, barely scraping through. I have to support my relatives more because of all this; I can't save much anymore.

I want to go back now. Or maybe work here for three more years and then go back, set up some shop, or maybe find a job in my kampong. But whenever I go back to Myanmar, within a month I want to come back. I miss Singapore. I can only make around 100–200 Singapore dollars a month in Myanmar. Working in Singapore allows me to have savings and support my mother and my girl.

Singapore has changed me. I have become stronger and more confident. I can *tahan*[8] anything. I'm no longer short-tempered like when I was young. One thing I'll take away from Singapore is happiness. In Myanmar people above forty feel ashamed to be happy; they don't mind their diet. People in Singapore live long, take care of their body and mental happiness. They happy-happy dancey-dancey. When I go back home, I want to take care of my happiness too. I have not been happy my whole life. Happiness is most important.

I don't know why I still want to go back to Myanmar. I'm not so close to my family there anyway . . . I still wonder why my eighty-year-old mother doesn't accept me till today, even though I pay for her expenses and even though the wives of my brothers she stays with complain so much about her. Maybe, I'm happy in Singapore but don't want to stay here forever. Myanmar is my country, my home. And then there is my little girl (brother's daughter). She treats me like her mother. I always call her. She is twenty now, studying International Policy in a good university. She has a boyfriend and I've never stopped her from having a relationship because I wish her to be happy. But now I just want her to be safe.

---

[8] Tolerate

After the coup, the army started arresting and killing young people. Many were shot, some went into hiding, and all universities were closed. I was at work when I saw the news of the army shooting a girl in Mandalay. My eyes went all black. My body started shaking and I burst into tears. I couldn't work. My customer complained to my boss that I forgot many things. I had to explain that there were problems in my family. I worry so much for my little girl now. Like other young people, she is also hiding. But I think the young should not stop protesting, because there are many problems in Myanmar. The army killed many, the big shots took all the money; the young find no work after studies; the elderly die early.

Because of Myanmar's bad economic situation, there are many broken families, and as a result, many orphans. Some live in shelters and some stay with their grandparents. Sometimes I give money to a lady running an orphanage. Many children there have been abandoned by their parents because they have some birth defects. But they are so nice . . . How can the parents throw them away? I dream of building my own place to house orphans and I'm trying to save money for this dream, so that others won't have a childhood like mine.

I Saw the First Half of My Life in My Lungs X-ray

Chen Nian Xi (China), fifty-two years old, Miner, Writer, former domestic migrant worker in China

I grew up in a small village in Shanxi. The 2,000-people village, nestled deep in the mountains, stretched along the fifty kilometre-long Xiahe River. My strongest childhood memory is hunger. It was the era of cooperatives with food being rationed to families according to the hours they worked. There were many children in my family but few working adults. We never had enough to eat. Like a reflex, till today I treasure food very much. I will never order too much when eating out and always pack the leftovers.

I saw a town only when I was twenty, even though it was just seventy kilometres from my village. There was no public transport and few of us had even seen a bicycle. So any villager who had been to the town was treated like a hero. With 1 yuan in my pocket, I arrived at the town on the back of a lorry amidst flying dust. Saving some for the return fare, I spent every cent of the rest on books: *Count of Monte Cristo*, *Three Musketeers*, Chinese literary magazines. On the way back, I read hungrily, treasuring every word, every moment of reading.

Those days everyone wanted to read. We had no TV. With limited information from outside, newspapers and books were cherished. Even the poor spent on newspapers. One news report titled *Through smoke and fire in Da Xing An Ling*—a very detailed account of a forest fire—is still alive in my memory. There were such vivid details such as the wild boars running and getting burnt into meatballs by the gushing fire. I admired writers and journalists so much.

Living in those remote high mountains, I was ignorant. I thought the world was as small as what I saw. I never thought of studying in a university or doing business—those options were not known to me—I just wanted to make some money to buy what I liked, for example, biscuits. Back then, the shops stocked very few things: oil, salt, only one type of biscuit. Those only available biscuits tasted so delicious. Only worth a few cents, those biscuits were my biggest desire. I have never eaten anything so good. Maybe it's easier to be happy when desires and needs are simple. Like we hardly had any warm clothes. During the bitter cold winters, we sat by the fire at home burning from the dry woods we collected. How blissful it was to be by that fireside!

A relative introduced me to mining work. My first tasks were to carry tons of waste out of the caves. After that I worked as a mine blaster for sixteen years, in many mines across China. I frequented a gold mine in Henan province. It was a big project and is operating even today. Whenever I couldn't find any other work, I went there. The mine stretched around 200 kilometres long, surrounding the Qin Ling Mountains. I knew many people there. The area was full of people: workers, small-time traders, food sellers . . . This 'Army of 100,000 people' was looking for gold and a bowl of rice. It was hard to walk through them. Mine workers like me moved around with small hammers and drills. There was a giant rock in the middle of nowhere on which someone was bored enough to carve the words *Xing Fu Lu*[9]. Later, someone else was also bored enough to paint it in red. These words could be seen from far and the rock became a meeting point for

---

[9] Happiness Road

us. Everyone had rested on it. We talked about Happiness Road when we called home.

The world inside the mines was complex. Caves were linked to one another, sometimes stretching up to ten kilometres. Some caves climbed up the mountains while some dived down through earth. Inside their monotonous structure, we lost our bearings quickly. Mere few kilometres felt like never-ending and dreadful. Our steps, 'thump, thump, thump' sounded louder and louder. The occasional sound of water-drops was deafening. It made me feel like I was nothing more than a small stone in this nether world. Inside, I felt all alone, powerless and scared.

In this maze, some lost their way and stumbled into abandoned caves. Tragedy struck when their torch ran out of batteries. They got lost and died slowly from lack of oxygen. Sometimes we chanced upon their dead bodies. I too lost my way at times. Luckily, as a blaster I was familiar with explosion patterns on the wall. Tracing such patterns by hand, I managed to navigate out of the darkness.

I didn't think much about these dangers. If I died, I would have no regrets. I had no debt, no credit; I always cleared everything when I moved. But dear oh dear! Did my wife suffer back home? Whenever she heard the crows calling, she became extremely nervous[10].

Back in the 1990s, the mining caves were dug low to keep costs down. With my height of five feet eleven inches, I couldn't even raise my head when inside. My back was bent for the whole day. I worked eight to ten hours a day, but sometimes up to fifteen when the machine was down, or when the rock was hard to penetrate. Deep inside, no fresh air could enter. I got headaches from the high concentration of carbon dioxide. Whether I was fully drenched in sweat or I was extremely hungry, I had no choice but to keep working. There was no food inside, and we could never leave halfway for food. Somehow, we also never thought of carrying food with us. I don't know where I found all the strength to carry on. I can't imagine how I endured all this for sixteen years. Those days we were young and thought we were

---

[10] Crows' calling in China means a bad omen

almighty. Overtime, such irregular food habits caused many miners to have gastric disease.

Thinking back, my sixteen years of working as a blaster was like a purgatory. I didn't make much money, none of us did. But I got many things out of it: lost hearing in one ear, severe cervical spine problem, rheumatism . . . all the occupational diseases of a mine worker, you name it. My miner brother was diagnosed with pneumoconiosis; he can now work only as a rickshaw driver. An ex-colleague died of stage-II pneumoconiosis last year. Until he died, he couldn't even lie flat to rest. Now it has found me. I remember looking at my X-ray report; I saw the first half of my life in it.

I was the happiest when I could bring money home. Once, my brother and I made 10,070 yuan each, working in Tongguan for three months. This stash of cash, in lump sum, felt so large, something we had never seen. Both of us thought it would be amazing to surprise our wives by giving them this entire stash of cash. Determined to not break it, we reached home spending only the 70 yuan we had separately, foregoing all food and drinks for the entire trip. Each of us gave the 10,000 yuan bundles to our wives with big drama. We were overjoyed. It was such a precious moment.

But the toughest part was dealing with the uncertainties in life as an itinerant migrant worker. You make some money in one place, and then nothing in the next. Sometimes, there was no work. Some other times, there was only work, no money.

One time, a few of us went to Gansu to work. The mining company gave us handmade explosives; they were useless to break the rocks. We decided to leave. On our way out, the van broke down and we got trapped for eleven hours. Because we didn't get paid, we had very little money. I had only 20 yuan, only enough for either one bowl of noodles or a one-night stay in a hotel. We debated among ourselves: food or sleep? In the end, we chose the noodles.

Another time, in 2010, I was called upon to go to Tian Shan, Xinjiang, right after Chinese New Year. I spent 9,000 yuan, travelled by bus from one end of China to another; through snow and ice. In the end, I made no money. The work conditions were dire. Ten of us worked concurrently with ten drilling machines. Dust blocked our sight, entered our airways, made us vomit. For seven days, we worked like this. We thought we were going to die. The boss didn't allow us to leave till we repaid his 2,000 yuan each for our transport. Our families sent us some money and we could finally leave after working for ten more days. As I left, I threw away my work overalls and boots on the mountain top. This coverall and boots followed me to many places that year; and that whole year I didn't earn anything. I swore that I'd never work in this industry again. (Now, as you can see, I didn't honor my words after that.)

My colleagues and I were comrades-in-arms. Our common enemies were the rocks; our common goal was to make money. We celebrated when we found good metals, even though this wealth never belonged to us. Today, some of them have left this world while some are suffering from diseases. Some continue to work in the mines, even going to faraway places like Indonesia and Africa. But we have not drifted apart. Our friendship remains solid. But many are no longer around.

Once, I teamed up with Wang Er, a technically savvy miner. When we encountered an extremely stubborn rock that drillers could not work through, we decided to explode it. Our young assistant brought us a pack of explosives, a detonator and a fuse. Wang Er cut off half of the fuse and threw the rest to the assistant, 'Half is enough, you wastrel!' Wang Er tried to light the fuse but failed nearly twenty times. His hands were shaking. Then there was a big explosion. When I woke up, I had lost the hearing in my right ear. Wang Er was dead.

I have worked in many mines, but rarely interacted with the locals anywhere. After all, a mine is a world of its own.

One winter, I went to Fushun to work. By April the weather was becoming hot, but I only had warm clothes to wear and was yet to receive my salary. I tried to borrow 10 yuan from a local who worked in the mining office. When he heard my reason for borrowing, he offered me one of his shirts instead. I said, 'You are so much shorter, how can I fit in your clothes?' He said he would give me an oversized shirt he got from his niece's clothing store when it shut down. True enough, he gave me a shirt that was too big even for me. I realized that this shirt was actually expensive. When I tried to pay him back later, he refused.

With locals, one has to be careful anyway. One of my colleagues went to Yarkand, where drunken locals roamed around aimlessly, always carrying a knife for carving meat. There he got involved in a fight between locals, got stabbed and then hospitalized for a long time. So I am always scared in unfamiliar places.

Once I worked near the Yarkand River in Southern Xinjiang. This small town of 3,000 people was the strangest place I have seen. There were no Hans there, all Uighur and Kashgar. Few spoke any Mandarin. I was curious how they lived: there was no grass to graze, no soil to plant, and yet no one went out for work. They were probably illiterates. In the evenings, the locals sat chatting in a row under the poplar trees. Like real masters, they sang and danced to the dombra[11]. I was mesmerized how music had taken roots in their hearts.

I underwent a major spinal surgery in 2015. After that, my body could no longer support my working in the mines. My wife tended the farmland back home, but it was not enough to support our life and my son's education. I worked as a copywriter in Guizhou; I also worked as a lyric writer for singers competing in live television shows. These were 'trendy' stuff and I found it hard to catch up with this modern society, having worked in mines for half my life. I spent three months in Beijing learning to write lyrics.

Now I have some writing gigs[12], some income, and some friends. My life has a little more freedom but is a bit dull. I have little desires and little worries. I am fifty years old. Fifty is when one knows his fate and the pointlessness of fighting it. Our life's possibilities are determined by how and where we are born. We miners at the bottom of society have this fatalistic outlook because we tried but failed many times to escape life's patterns.

Could I have lived differently? If I had known better, I would not have gambled my life for sixteen years. All I have won is a long list of complicated diseases.

---

[11] Musical instrument popular in Xinjiang

[12] *By Feb 2022, Chen has published three books that have become top sellers in China.*

Part II

How do political conditions in one's home country force a person to become a migrant worker? How dire does situation at home need to be to make a person overcome the fear and uncertainty of the foreign land? Is the act of migration essentially a gamble? Does this also make some migrant workers habitual gamblers? Is planning for the future too much of a luxury for a migrant worker? Where can a 'stateless' migrant worker anchor one's identity and preserve a sense of belonging?

In this section, the featured migrant workers—Niroj, Khagendra, Lalim (Nepal); Dilip (India); and Aomsin and Mai (Myanmar)—dwell on these questions and more as they narrate their life stories.

I Used to Fight in a War. Now I Salute in Condominiums

Nepalese security guards in Malaysia

A little shy, a little hesitant, quite a bit out of place; unmistakably visible with their uniforms—sometimes a cowboy attire, sometimes a fluorescent mesh jacket, or a white shirt with shoulder straps—Nepalese security guards are conspicuous all over Malaysia, forming the frontline and the rear-guard; in shopping malls, condominiums, parking lots, and corporate towers.

* * *

Niroj, 25

I come from Phulwa, a village near the Indian border, near Darjeeling. I have been in Malaysia for more than a year.

I work twelve hours every day, seven days a week. There are no holidays for us. I work from 8 a.m. till 8 p.m. but my shift timing changes every fifteen days.

I came here after paying 200,000 Nepalese rupees[13] to the agent in Nepal. For this, I have taken a loan at 30 per cent interest. Here I

---

[13] ~1,700 US Dollars

get 1,500 ringgit every month as salary. Then my boss also gives me 200 ringgit for food and another 100 ringgit for calling home. And I get to stay in a dormitory nearby. Every month, I send home 500 ringgit.

I used to work as a policeman in Nepal. I left them because I ran into some problems with my colleagues there. And a policeman's salary in Nepal isn't good at all.

Most Nepalese security guards in Malaysia are ex-army or policemen from Nepal. There are so many of us here. Every building is guarded by a Nepali. In any building in Malaysia, the first person you will see is a Nepali.

But there are many illegals; some claim to have worked in Nepal army or Nepal Police but in their whole life they haven't even chased a mosquito. And then there are these Pakistanis also. You can't believe it, brother. They put on name tags like Ram Bahadur or Ram Singh. Imagine! They are Muslims and then they take on these Hindu names so shamelessly. You can easily catch them by the way they speak. There are two types of Nepali security guards in Malaysia; the Nepali-Nepali and the cheaper ones, the Pakistani Nepali.

The guardroom is my office. It is so small. I have no chair. There are pictures of Mothers[14] all over the walls. These are not mine. My boss is a Hindu man. He is a good man. There was a Bangladeshi guard here sometime back, illegal of course. He was Muslim but would not mind these pictures. He was a good man. I heard he was caught by the police and sent back. Sometimes I hear that the Malaysian government will change the law and send us Nepalis back also. What have we done wrong?

When my duty is over, I just go home, eat, wash clothes, sleep, then cook, then get ready to come here. There is nothing much we can do. Every day is like this. See these CCTVs; they are my TV (entertainment). It is strange but time just passes even if I just watch these.

Boring, boring, life here is so boring.

I can stay here for another two years. Maybe I can save enough to get married. If I can't, I will have to apply again to come back. Everyone here is so rude. Especially, some of these contractors

---

[14] Hindu goddesses

who come here (for repair work) are so rude. When we ask which apartment they need to go to and if they have a written permit they speak in bad language just because we are foreigners. I can't wait to go back.

It is 8 a.m., the time to change guards. The newcomer, Khagendra, takes off his denim jacket. Niroj puts on a denim jacket. Khagendra puts on a cap. Niroj takes off his cap. Niroj hands over his walkie-talkie to Khagendra. The ceremony is over.

* * *

Khagendra, 35

I have been working in Malaysia for over five years with breaks in between. I used to be in the army but had left it after a short stint. The Maoists were after us. They attacked only when they knew that we were outnumbered and they could kill us all. At the army, every day was full of anxiety. When will we get ambushed? Today? Tomorrow? I had a wife and a daughter. The pay was not worth it. I couldn't stay long.

Compared to Nepal, there is hardly much work here. See, we need to be really good at pressing this button to open the gate, like this. And, we also need to know how to give a good salute when one of the resident's cars passes by. Let me give you a demo. Since I am from the army, I do it well.

Then I have to maintain this visitor's register. See. This is my list of Facebook friends.

In all my five years as a guard here, I have never seen any theft or anything more violent. Of course, if something bad happens, then it will be a big problem.

I know only a few words of Malay[15] only. Once I wished a man 'Selamat Mati' instead of 'Selamat Pagi'. That's Happy Death and not Good Morning. I can't explain the man's reaction!

* * *

---

[15] Bahasa Melayu

Lalim, 37

What can I tell you (about Nepal)? So much has happened. So many big words. So many promises. So many have died. And in the end it's still the same. The rich are getting richer. The same politicians are getting even richer. Maoists, Nepali Congress there is no difference.

In my army days, I wondered if I would see my wife and daughter again. I was scared of dying. But as I am here now, I haven't been with them anyway. It has been three years. I send them all my money, yet I feel like I have become so distant from my family, like we are no longer close. And I am scared that they feel the same way too.

Now I Feed the Same People Who Destroyed Our Village

Shillong, with its agreeable highland weather, is where everyone in North-East India goes to when it comes to studying at posh boarding schools, checking out the latest fashion, and escaping the heat of all the political turmoil of the region. But this major cosmopolitan centre not only attracts the rich kids of politicians, businessmen and insurgents; but also a large pool of migrant workers. The Khasis—a matrilineal people who claim to be more indigenous than others in the region—have often erupted into violence, forming their own armed gangs who terrorized the 'outsiders'.

* * *

Dilip, twenty-three, runs a street-side momo shop (on contract basis) in one of the narrow lanes that climb uphill from Shillong's city centre. He came to Shillong with his wife from the neighbouring state of Tripura.

Dilip

We came a few years back when things were too violent in Tripura. Same like everywhere here, locals fighting the outsiders, the Bengalis. Both sides had guns and killed each other without even looking at their faces. It was hard to get a job. So we came to Shillong and started selling momos. The Bengalis controlled everything in Tripura. The local people became like farm animals, like cows and dogs. You can't have that for too long. Same thing happened here in Shillong also.

Business here is good when the tourists come. The Bengalis love these momos. But it feels strange because in Tripura it was the Bengalis who destroyed our village. Now my business runs on them. I know everyone is the same; all men are good, all men are bad. But imagine if you let me come into your house and then I start bossing around and make you eat my leftovers. And I do this for years and years. Will you not want to throw me out of your house then?

I have a hobby. I bet. There is this archery contest that happens here every evening. It is mainly for betting. My wife scolds me, saying it is a bad habit. But I have made some money there, haven't I, wife? You also feel happy when I win, right?

You have to bet on many numbers, essentially you bet on how many arrows will hit the target. So you can't just bet one rupee or ten rupee, no point. You must bet around 1,000 rupees if you want to win some. A few times, I even made 500,000. Haven't I, wife? When I win big, I pretend that I lost it all so that I don't get robbed later. But everyone knows within a few days. They say if you bet one rupee, you have a one in hundred chance of making eighty rupees. That's so much better than praying to God, right?

Maybe someday we will go back to Tripura for good. Or maybe we will go somewhere else. Things are fine here as it is. But maybe someday the people here will turn against us like they did with the Nepalis recently. I have run away once. I can run away again.

I Don't Know My Future,
Do You Know Yours?

Aomsin (Myanmar), twenties, Sex worker in Thailand

I was born in Shan state in Myanmar. We are three brothers and three sisters. My parents were farmers. But my father was taken away by the Myanmar army to work for them as a porter. He escaped to Thailand and started working there. The rest of my family came later to join him. In Thailand, my parents worked as day labourers in farms, sometimes in lychee plantations, sometimes in garlic or onion farms.

When I came to Thailand, I was about eight years old. So that was about two years ago. No, no, (laughs), maybe over twenty years. I remember that we walked for three or four days to the border and then some people put us in a truck. There were many boxes filled with cabbage in the truck. So we became like cabbage. My family had to pay a lot to sit in that truck. They dropped us in the middle of the night on top of a mountain. We had to hide there overnight before we could come down to find a way to get into the town.

I was a normal kid, eat, play, sleep. In Myanmar, I was going to school. But in Thailand, I had to start my schooling again from the beginning, through distance learning. I stopped studying after middle-high school and started working. I really wanted to study, but life just didn't make it possible. I believe everyone should have some basic education. So many years later, I joined Empower, our sex worker organization, which runs education programmes. There, I finished my high school. I studied because I just wanted to be smarter.

As a child, I was always at home, taking care of my siblings and doing housework. On weekends, I went to work, peeling garlic. I was about nine or ten years old then. I also made some money pulling grass from agricultural fields. Then I started working in the kitchen of a noodle restaurant. It was ridiculous. They made me work like twelve or fourteen hours a day, for nothing, you know, very low salary. So I quit and took up the job of looking after an old person. After that, I became a domestic helper[16] with a family close to that old person. That work was good but my elder sister needed help in her restaurant in Bangkok so I went there. This was almost like a twenty-four hour job, not just at the restaurant but also at the house. It was too much. So I came back home and began working in a tofu shop. Here again, the hours were long and the pay was very little. So I began serving beer in a small pub. And then some friends said, if you do the same work in a karaoke instead, you will get a much bigger salary. So I joined a karaoke bar. The conditions weren't so good in that place. After some time, I joined a Go Go bar. That is where I became a sex worker.

In my life, I have done so many things. In all these places, I learnt a lot of things. Now I live in Chiang Mai; my family lives in the neighbouring district. Their house is not on the mountain but they can see the mountain.

As a sex worker, I have more freedom and have to work less hours. Most customers are good men with very respectable jobs and they are very polite. For those customers who are not, we spread the word very quickly amongst all the sex workers, 'Don't go with this guy. He's fussy, he's mean or whatever'. There are violent customers only in the movies, documentaries, and in the news. Yeah, I understand that

---

[16] Some migrant workers in the domestic services sector prefer to be called as domestic workers. The words 'helper' or 'maid' can also be seen in this book if the featured worker has chosen these words herself.

the media has to sell the news so they make it sensational, but in our community, there is not so much violence we hear of.

Earlier, I was the main breadwinner for my family. I built them a house. I also paid for the education of my brothers and sisters. Now that all that is done, I have already reduced the amount I send each month to my family. But since COVID, I can't send anything. All Go Go bars are closed. There are no tourists also. I try to make do by selling lottery, waitressing, whatever I can do. Sometimes I get some money for doing outreach or other work for our movement. But it has been hard. My savings are shrinking fast. I have many people behind me—my family—to take care of. I can only afford to help buy them something sometime but I am unable to send any regular payment back home.

I am sure that my parents know about my work. Because they're very smart people, not stupid. But everyone doesn't need to know every detail. Like, okay, they also knew that at one stage, I was a domestic worker, but they didn't need to know how I scrubbed the floor or what kind of washing up I did. It's the same for sex work. You don't need to know all the details. I'm sure the funeral director doesn't tell every detail of his work to his family.

Yeah, I went back once to my hometown, a long time after we had left. Going back was just a one day trip from the border. There's a road now. It's not a three day walk anymore. Once I was planning to use some of my savings to buy a home in Shan state. And then I imagined that I would have one home in Thailand and one home in Shan state. But with the recent military coup and the war going on, I stopped thinking about that. You know, we like all the local food here in Thailand, we work here, do everything here,, but in my heart I feel that I am Shan. Maybe In terms of legal nationality, I want to be a Thai, but in terms of my heart, Shan. But then . . . actually sometimes in my heart I feel Thai . . .

Do locals discriminate against me? It depends on how much money I am paying in shops or other places. If I pay well, they all treat me the same way as they treat their local customers. But the police are a different matter altogether. Sometimes I have to pay the police just for being someone travelling as a migrant. If I want to go anywhere, I have to ask for permission, even if it is only one hour away. Once I visited my family without getting permission. On the way, the police took all my money.

What can I say about my future plans? I'm a normal kind of person. In my free time, I watch movies, sleep, listen to music, go home and visit my parents . . . or shopping, clothes or gold (laughs) . . . So as any normal kind of person, yeah, one day I do want to have my own family. But it's not something I'm looking for or something that I'm avoiding. I will need to keep working until I don't need money or gold anymore. But I may change jobs. If I stop working, life will be so boring. So even if I didn't need the money or the gold, I will probably still do something. The last two years have been very boring without any work. Yeah. It has been a long holiday.

I have a dream; that on the first and fifteenth of every month—the day the lottery comes—I win the lottery. Then I will use that money to buy a big house and buy some more land. Then I want to come to Singapore. Should I tell you the truth? I am now a stateless person. So before my dream comes true, I first need to get some kind of travel document, so it's a long way.

Anyway, people without a country don't ever get any retirement pension. They have to work till they die, yeah. I am not sure, I don't know about my future. How about you? Do you know your future?

I Wish to Find Out Everything the World has to Offer

Mai (Myanmar), thirties, Sex worker in Thailand

I was born in Shan state in Myanmar. My parents were farmers. We have many boys in the family, four sons. I also have two sisters. There, the Burmese army would come and take our sons to join in the army. The army made sure that each family gave two or three of their sons. These men just died. My parents didn't want this to happen to their own sons. And so they left to come to Thailand.

When we came to Thailand, I was a little girl, maybe five years old. That was about thirty years ago. I came walking through the jungle with my family. Sometimes my father carried me on his back but sometimes my little legs had to walk, walk, walk. We crossed a small river; that was the border. On the boat, they told us not to talk. They asked me to hold my breath. My parents said that if I speak or breathe, the boat will topple over. All the way, I tried to hold my breath. All I remember is how tired I was.

Here, my father and brothers worked as day labourers in agricultural farms and also as construction workers. When I was a child, I rarely went out. I was always at home minding my younger siblings because my parents were working. So I had become their babysitter. I also did all the washing and cooking. So literally, I was like a housewife.

35

I never had any proper schooling. In Myanmar, my mother had taken me to a school once. I didn't like it there. I felt threatened by the teacher. I ran away and refused to ever go back after that first day. In Thailand, my parents had to move for work continually. So they never put me in school here.

But I was the kind of kid that liked to learn things. I was so curious to know everything. For example, I was really determined to be able to write very beautifully and I didn't of course have any paper, pen or pencil. But I had a stick and I had dirt so I practiced writing in the dirt until my writing became beautiful. I was very curious whenever anybody came to our house; I liked to sit and listen to what the grown-ups talked about. My mother used to shoo me away but I would still stay and listen to whatever they discussed.

I did a lot of my learning on my own. When my family moved to Chiang Mai, I asked my mother if I could go to study at the distance learning programme run by the Thai government. Thereafter, I joined the education program run by Empower, the sex worker organization. There, I finished my high school. This time I didn't feel as threatened. So I didn't run away.

I began my working life by washing dishes at a resort. I was only sixteen then. I would give all my money to my mother, for the family. Then I worked for a long time alongside my father in the National Park. When I was twenty-one, my mother died. So I decided to leave home and find a better paying job. I went to Bangkok and started working with my extended family, selling fruits and fruit juice. That business didn't go well. I came back to Chiang Mai and joined a massage business run by another extended family. I found that I can't really give massage, I just didn't have the strength. So I took a job in a bakery. The boss there was really fussy so I left the bakery as well. Eventually I got a job in a bar, and then in a snooker hall, and then in a Go Go bar. It was at the snooker hall that I began doing sex work with the customers.

Our customers are mainly men, some women. Most are Westerners, some other Asians and a very few Thai men. Where I work, the Go Go bars, they don't allow Thai men to come in. Are we afraid of our customers? Well, we are more afraid of not having customers, of not working. Of course, there are fussy customers and stingy customers. They're the ones we don't go with once we know their nature. Regarding violent customers, I haven't met any; and we all know very well stories of women who face violence from their boyfriends and husbands instead, not from customers.

As a sex worker, my income comes from a few sources. When a customer buys me an alcoholic drink, I get a commission. When we're dancing at the Go Go bar, the tips that the customers give us; that's our money, we don't share it with the bar. When we go with the customer, we keep what the customer pays us; we don't share that with the bar either. The customer has to pay the bar a smaller amount to be able to go with us. In some places, the sex workers are on a salary. But when you're on that salary, there are a whole lot of rules like what hours you work so most sex workers would think it's not worth it.

I send money to my father every month, but only a small portion of my income. Most of the money that I was earning before COVID, I would put into savings and with that savings I was buying a lot of gold.

Because of COVID, all business has stalled. All bars are closed. I got double bad luck because I had a very serious motorcycle accident and I was just recovering and going back to work when COVID fell upon us. As I am also the main provider for my family, a lot of my savings has been used up. All that gold I had bought is what is getting us all through now. I have cut down on my cost of living. Before COVID, I was making 60,000 to 80,000 baht a month. Now I have only 20,000 baht left so if I have to try and live within that 20,000.

As for the locals, common people treat us very well. They see us as humans like them. They treat us just the same. As for fellow sex workers, the situation for sex work is not the same as other work. You usually don't see locals doing the typical work that migrants do. But in sex work, there are many locals also. In our workplace, there are many Thai women, indigenous women, all working alongside migrants, all mashed up together. Sometimes, we—Thai and migrants—even go together with the same customers.

The main problem for us comes from the government bureaucrats and the police. We face a lot of discrimination from them. For example, most recently and clearly, when the government was providing relief for people who had lost their jobs because of COVID, they did not include any migrant workers because they say we're aliens. And they say that the money is only for the Thai people so these aliens don't need to eat until COVID is gone! Yeah, let us be the ones to die first.

Also my ID card says that I am someone who comes from the highlands. We say it means that I live in a penthouse, ha ha. Well, my card says I don't have a country and I have no possibility of going back to my home country. Because of this ID, if I want to leave my area, I have to get permission. At one point, we couldn't even move outside the district but now we can move within the province. There are also many restrictions on work and other things because of this. So sometimes when I go out for business or something, they ask for my ID card which is normal practice. But when they see my ID card, their whole attitude changes. How they deal with me changes. They feel that they're immediately superior to me. They often ask us for money to let us travel. The rules keep changing.

Moreover, in Thailand, it is against the law to take money for sex.[17] So yes, every entertainment place in Thailand is paying the police. Usually the owner will pay and he collects the money from the women later. So people like me end up paying twice.

I joined Empower because I have always been that person wanting to know what's going on, remember? At Empower, I saw a group of women all doing different things so I wanted to join all those things. Actually I really believe that if we don't fight for ourselves then who's going to fight for us? We're going to have to do it ourselves. And the number one thing I want to change is to see the prostitution law gone.

Now I live alone in a rented apartment. My room is tiny but the place is close to the market, close to food, close to Empower.

---

[17] 'Sex work is practiced openly in Thailand, but it is illegal and subject to fines or, in rare cases, imprisonment. About 24,000 people were arrested, fined or prosecuted in 2019, according to the Royal Thai Police.' https://www.npr.org/sections/goatsandsoda/2021/02/03/960848011/how-the-pandemic-has-upended-the-lives-of-thailands-sex-workers#:~:

My family lives very close to where I live. In my free time, I go and visit them. I like shopping but there is no money for that now. No money, no honey.

Do you ask domestic workers if their families know about their work? A lot of domestic workers from Myanmar in Singapore don't want their family to know what they do, they lie, they find it very shameful. But people only ask us this question. The question comes from a point of view that selling sex is something shameful that you wouldn't want your parents to know or if they know they will feel ashamed. And so this question comes from that bias in the first place, so it's hard to answer. But yeah, my family knows that I work in a Go Go bar.

Now, am I more Thai or Shan? I feel like I am straddling between the two. On one hand, I think I deserve and should have the rights that Thai people have in Thailand. But at the same time, I am not going to forget my heritage. I remember that I am Shan and I will never forget that I am Shan.

I went back to my hometown about ten years ago when I had saved up enough money. I needed to take my father with me to do some documents. We went to take a look at our old house. There was nothing left. In Myanmar, I felt like I was very rich because there is a big difference between the economic condition of Thailand and Myanmar; everything there was so cheap compared to here. I felt like I had so much money. I thought about going back to Shan for good but how could you live there when the standard of living is so poor? There's no work there. And the government will just do things like cut the internet; they're still fighting there.

I can't see any future at the moment. The economy is just getting worse and worse. Our customers can't come to Thailand anymore because of the COVID restrictions. It has been 460 days since the bars were closed. Some sex workers in their early twenties are trying to go online. But online platforms and spaces are not really set up well in Thailand. Most of the customers are old guys, you know, they can't even take a photo on their phone, let alone use an online platform. So the future is a little bit bleak at the moment but if things recover then

I will do sex work until I can't do this anymore and then probably change to other jobs but I'm not sure what or how. I have no plans to stop selling whatever I can sell.

Regarding starting my family, I will just go with the flow. If it happens that there is a relationship and then a family, then that will happen on its own. It's not really a goal for me but is not something I am avoiding either.

I have a dream that I will have enough money, from the lottery, or somehow, to give to my father so that he never has to worry for the rest of his life. I want to buy a big house. Then with the rest of the money, I will go around the world as a tourist. I always had a dream of going to Switzerland, which I have already been to. Now I want to go to Vietnam, and then the whole world. I wish to find out everything in the world, just as I wanted since I was a little kid.

Part III

Many migrant workers view their act of migration as a sacrifice. A part of them constantly weighs their losses against their gains—is it all worthwhile? How does this idea of sacrifice shape the life of a migrant worker? How do they cope with the feeling of guilt arising out of separation from their most beloved ones, their children? But do their families actually exploit them in return?

In this section, the featured migrant workers—Lovely Comavig, Elpidia Abel Malicsi, Joan Santilan (The Philippines); Waruni Nimalka Perera (Sri Lanka); Erin Cipta (Indonesia); and Sagar (Bangladesh)—dwell on these questions and more as they narrate their life stories.

My Husband Put a Knife to My Neck

Lovely Comavig (The Philippines), twenty-nine years old,
Domestic Worker, worked in Saudi Arabia, currently
working in Singapore

I was born in the Southern Philippines. I was the only child. My father is a driver. My mother is a homemaker.

When I was four years old, we moved to the Marikina district in Manila. There was jungle everywhere in Marikina, even around my school. When it rained, the neighbourhood became a big lake.

Estrada was the President of the Philippines at that time and law enforcement was not strict. In Marikina, we heard of rape cases where the bodies of the victims were then found in the jungles . . . There were lots of drug dealings in the area. Many children were lost. A van could come out of nowhere to take you in; the gangsters then cut your tummy.

My childhood was very boring. My parents were scared of leaving me alone. I was not allowed to go out, not even allowed to take *jeepneys*[18]. I had no friends. My uncle dropped me to and from school. I just watched TV all day. I just had a little fun dancing in school as a cheerleader.

---

[18] Public transport in the Philippines

When I was twelve, I went out once without telling my mother. I wanted to know what 'outside' was like. A twenty something guy almost abducted me and took me to the jungle. Luckily, some people caught him.

After I finished high school, I refused to continue my studies. I was bored of studying. I wanted to enjoy life. My aunt said, 'Okay, if you don't go school, soon you'll become helper, soon you'll become pregnant.' I got so mad at her and said, 'It's okay if I become helper. Helper is a good job also! You have a daughter too. May your daughter become pregnant earlier!' Her daughter—my cousin—was a college graduate. And yes, what I said turned out to be true. She indeed became pregnant first!

I dreamed of working in a big ship or a hotel, as a cook. I liked cooking. But my parents said that I wouldn't find such jobs without hospitality training. They wanted me to go for nursing training. Many of my relatives working as nurses in Canada or in Massachusetts also offered to help me get there if I was willing to. But I didn't like this nursing nursing stuff.

During evacuation before Typhoon Ondoy, I met a man who was helping out with the rescue efforts. He was in his twenties. He was good to me. He would carry my bags. We started seeing each other. I didn't mind that he was older than me. He had a wife and a child before, but I never thought of asking about his situation. I was only sixteen. My parents didn't know about him. They were busy cleaning up our flooded house; didn't have time for me. I had full freedom. I ran away with my boyfriend.

At his home I was working like a helper. I never knew how to wash plates, clean the house. Being an only child, my mother never let me do any work. Soon, I felt sad and scared. I wanted to go back home but did not know how. I had no phone. I couldn't even contact my parents.

For three months, my boyfriend hid me at his place. My parents thought that I was dead. Eventually, my cousin told them the truth. Somehow, they managed to call his mother. Finally, we met again. They were angry that I had chosen a married man. My mother said, 'If you choose this man, I won't see your face again.' What she said was just out of anger.

Soon I had my first child. And then, the second. My husband began peddling drugs. One day, I was playing bingo with my friends. My eldest son was in my lap. Suddenly he began crying. Hearing his cries, my husband rushed in with a knife and yelled, 'You are not taking care of the baby!' My friends defended me but he still put the knife on my neck. I said, 'If you dare, just kill me!' My friends told my family about this incident. My dad went to the police. I didn't want this, because after all, he was my husband, my son's father. My mother said, 'It's not to put him in jail. We just filed a complaint in case anything happens to you.'

I was still in love with him back then.

Soon my husband was having an affair with a neighbour. She was also doing drugs. When I found out about the affair, the two of them confronted me. My husband went mad with anger. He took out a gun . . . shot at me . . . the bullet came out . . . I saw the light come to me like this . . . (gesture)

This is my second life now. (laughs)

I wanted to breakup and go back to my family. He said he'd change, and asked me to go with him and live with his parents in Bulacan. I was very angry but I was still in love. I was scared my family would be broken. I thought Bulacan would be nice because there won't be any drugs. I took my children and went with him. But no! Also a lot (drugs) there! Many big-time rich people got him to buy drugs in Marikina and sell them in Bulacan . . . I didn't ask him to stop . . .

One day, I asked him for money for milk powder for our babies. I didn't have a job . . . Other than drugs, he worked sometimes as a tricycle driver. When I asked for money for my babies' milk, he gave me just 10 pesos, only enough to buy one sachet of milo . . . (crying) I cried . . . 'How can this be enough? . . . Only half for one baby? . . . Only half for the other baby? . . . This is not enough . . . I better go to my family . . . we stop the relationship . . . ' He began beating me with a wooden plank. I couldn't fight . . . when I fought, he beat me even more . . . He took me behind the house and beat me real hard . . . I said you better take the knife and kill me now! My babies saw me . . . One was five and the other one was three years old . . . They screamed,

'Stop! My mama is going to die! . . . Don't do this . . . ' He caught them like this, by their throats, (violent gesture) and threw them away.

That moment I told myself, 'Lovely, wake up. This is not right. It is okay if he beats you . . . but if he beats your babies, this is not nice already.'

Secretly, I called my mother, asking her to send me some money. I told my husband that I was going for a short visit to my parents. I didn't take any clothes or belongings. I dressed simply, took the children along, and came to Manila.

After going back to my parents, I worked as a cashier in a convenience store, but the money was not even enough for milk and diapers for my kids. My auntie suggested that I go to Saudi Arabia. I was scared . . . I refused. But my aunt secretly applied for my passport and then asked me to go for the appointment. I was still hesitating when one night my ex-husband came to hunt for me. I was at my relative's house then. That day, I decided to go out of the country, if only for a while.

I paid 1,400 pesos for a month-long training. They taught us how to do laundry, how to cook, how to arrange spoons, forks and glasses. I was very confused with so many spoons to arrange. I was scared of not passing the test. If so, I would have to pay for the tuition again. Somehow, I passed the exam and went to Saudi . . . only to find out that Saudis didn't use spoons, they just used hands to eat! (laughs)

I didn't let my family see me off at the airport. I didn't want to see my children cry. It was very painful and sad, almost like I was going to die, as if it was the last time we would be seeing each other. Since then I have always been away. I was only twenty-three then.

In Saudi, my employer had a family of fifteen; one husband, three wives, eleven children. My Ma'am was wife number two of the Baba[19]; she had six children. I was only supposed to serve my Ma'am and take care of her kids. The other wives didn't have helpers, maybe because only my Ma'am had a job, as a teacher. But the whole family hosted big

---

[19] Male employer in Saudi

parties on Fridays. When that happened, I had to work for the entire family as the only helper.

I woke up at 5 a.m. every day. On the dining table, there would often be a lot of dirty big plates already. They seemed to have big late night parties. Some nights, I would wake up from their noise, thinking they were not human, but monsters in the house. This was my 'breakfast' every day—washing a lot of things in the kitchen. I was very angry with their non-stop use of *Pangea*[20]. They used one cup after another, and then another again . . . They put the seeds of dates in the Pangea and would take a new cup again—every time so many cups to wash like this. After I made breakfast for the family, I cleaned the house and the toilets, then cooked three or four dishes. When the food was being cooked, I'd take a nap in the kitchen.. After the children came back from school at 12 p.m. and had lunch, I'd wash the plates, dishes, and all the uniforms. By then it would be 3 p.m. Then I had to make coffee and cakes for Baba and Ma'am, I had to serve dinner for all and then wait for them to finish eating so that I could wash the plates. And after dinner they'd ask me to make coffee again. It would be 11 p.m. or 12 a.m. by then already. I would call my family at 1 a.m. and then finally go to sleep. Even then, they often knocked on my door, 'Wake up, make tea, make *Qahwa*[21], make some biryani . . . some visitors have come.' I would say, 'I want to sleep, Ma'am'. She would say, 'I'll give you a rest day tomorrow.' But that tomorrow never came . . . I had no off-day. On some days I could only rest for one-two hours, especially during Ramadan.

Often I cried because I was very, very, tired. I thought of my mother, my father and my children. I asked myself why I was staying here. Why was I doing this? I had no rest but I became very fat . . . 85 kg . . . don't know why. I resented my ex-husband. If not for him, I would still be with my family, staying with my children to see them grow up. But then I remembered his gun.

My Arabic was terrible when I had just arrived. When people said 'thank you' in Arabic, I used to reply 'very much'. But I quickly learned how to speak the language.

---

[20] Small coffee cups
[21] Coffee

In Saudi, I had to always keep my hair covered, even after I had just finished bathing. I opened my hair once (in the hall) when nobody was there. Then Baba came from school and scolded me saying, 'If my kids see your hair, it's haram!' I couldn't make calls in the kitchen because I could be jailed if any woman in the house got seen by my father on the screen. I couldn't go out unless I was with my employers. I couldn't see the sun come out or go down. The windows were very dark so that people couldn't see our faces from outside, otherwise 'haram'. Whether it was in the airport or in the mall, everywhere there were only men, no women. When outside, I was scared. But when inside also, I was scared. I knew some employers had CCTV all over the house. I wore chador even in my room and looked everywhere. It was so hot . . . I was losing hair . . . When I went back to the Philippines, I had little hair.

My Ma'am went for women-only parties where they could all remove their head covers. They would call me to do up their hair and paint nails for parties. But they didn't give me time to change my clothes or shower when I went along. I just wore work clothes there. No, I had no time to take care of myself at all. But I never saw my Ma'am go for shower. There would be other helpers in such parties too. The Saudi people called us *Kadam*[22]. We Kadams laughed about our employers, 'They are all very pretty but they never shower!' Ma'am's sisters liked me because I was talkative. When they danced, they also invited me to dance. They looked for me when I was not at the party. The other helpers said I was very lucky because my Ma'am didn't treat me like a helper. I was laughing all the time although my sad life was always in my mind.

My Ma'am treated me well. But sometimes she borrowed money from me and returned only after a long time. Because of her daily parties and all the expensive gifts she bought, her money ran out fast.

Some helpers were not allowed to talk. An Indonesian said her employers didn't give her food. She only got leftovers. When I went to parties, I gave my food to them. I knew I could eat anything I wanted in

---

[22] Domestic Worker

my Ma'am's house. I was very sad for those who couldn't. The helpers would pack whatever was left in the party in plastic bags, as their food for the whole week.

One Ethiopian girl had bruises on her face. She cried, saying that her Baba beat her. A Filipino friend of mine; her Baba's son followed her into the toilet and tried to rape her. She ran and got a knife and said to him, 'I'll kill you if you do this to me.' Her Ma'am didn't believe her. Here, even if you don't do anything wrong, no one trusts you if you are just a helper. The employer sent her back to the Philippines. But she was lucky, because they could have sent her to jail for holding the knife.

I was also scared that my Baba's eldest son, from his first wife, might rape me. He always talked dirty like, 'You are yummy, better than this (food).' One day, during my rest time, he suddenly opened my door, 'Hi Filipina, Are you okay? Have you showered?' I scrambled to cover my hair. When my Ma'am moved me to a room outside the house, this man teased me, "You can bring your boyfriend there.' Ma'am told me to pretend that I didn't hear anything. The funny thing is that his wife got jealous of me because of his behaviour.

On the other hand, my Ma'am's sons always treated me with respect. If they gave me anything, they'd make sure not to touch my hand. But they were difficult in other ways, especially the young ones. Once, the youngest boy threw noodles at me. I just stared at him. I was feeling angry but I controlled myself. This was not my place.

My Ma'am's eldest daughter always demanded a lot, as if she was the number 1 person in the house. Always asked me to paint her nails, do her hair first . . . even if I needed to do work in the kitchen. As if I was running a salon (laughs). When she gave birth to a baby, they didn't know how to take care of it. They didn't shower the baby even if it smelt bad. When the baby felt cold, they still had air-conditioners switched on. I was very sad for this baby. They'd knock at my door at 3 a.m., asking me to look after the baby. Saudi people were bored with babies—they had too many. They just 'Mubarak-Mubarak'[23], played with the baby like a toy, and then nobody cared any more.

---

[23] Blessed

The mother was too young, only seventeen years old. She just gave me the baby whenever the husband was in the room. The women in Saudi were focused on their husbands only. She was the only wife then, and she was worried about the husband finding another wife. I was happy when she finally left with her husband for America.

As the second wife, my Ma'am was very jealous about the youngest wife. She used to send me to spy on her. If the other wife received new gifts, then my Ma'am would question Baba why he didn't give this to her. But I never reported anything, because I didn't want them to fight because of me.

When Baba talked to me about things like coffee, the ladies got jealous. Sometimes when the Baba sat with his three wives, he called me to also sit with them. I felt very embarrassed. It felt like I was 'the fourth wife'. I'd make excuses to go to the kitchen.

No, I'd never want to become the fourth wife . . . I'm a Filipina . . . I was twenty-four . . . If I became the fourth wife, all the other wives would gang up to bully me, or maybe even kill me. Haha.

Working in Saudi was good. I worked for my children. I didn't need to ask my ex-husband for any help. I could stand on my own feet. Yet, I didn't want to renew my contract. I was really tired after working so much every day for two years and four months.

As I was about to leave Ma'am's house, her youngest child asked me where I was going. I said I had to do something in the Philippines. He said, 'Then you just go there for one hour and come back.' He started crying and following me. I was so sad to leave him.

I wanted to go to Hong Kong. But I heard that employers there could terminate helpers for strange reasons like if they think the helper is not good for their house Feng shui. My best friend wanted to come to Singapore. I was a bit reluctant because for Singapore we had to pay agency fees. Still, I came along with her.

When I arrived in Singapore, I stayed for four days at the agency's place. They took away my phone. I couldn't contact my family and they didn't know what was happening to me. They made us do some work, but gave us so little food. It was spicy, I couldn't eat at all. Luckily, I had brought instant noodles. I shared my food with the other new helpers there.

For the first few months in Singapore, I had to repay the agency loan and had nothing left to send back home. I asked my ex-husband to help pay for our children's school uniform. He asked so many questions, 'What are you doing in Singapore, where's your money, you work there for what . . . you work with whom?'

From then on, I have never asked him for any money.

Till now my babies don't like talking to their father. If the father calls, they'll just say, 'Hi,' 'Hello'. The father accuses me for brainwashing his sons and bad-mouthing him. I said, 'I didn't brainwash. I'm fair to my sons. Ask your sons why they don't want you.'

When I had just gone to Saudi, my eldest son had asked me on the phone, 'Mama where are you?' I said, 'I go to work.' He said, 'You go to papa already? He will kill you!'

The children remember what they saw.

My first child was only five years old when I left for Saudi. When he asked me for something and I didn't give him fast enough, he'd blame me, 'I hope you are not my mother. I hope you die there. Why did God give you as my mother?' So painful. I'm scared that they'll say such things even after they grow up. But what can I do? If I stay with them, I cannot provide what they need. If I go back, and if my father has no work, then we'll all die. Nobody will help us.

They don't understand that I sacrificed to give them what they want. But I'm still sorry.

Now, I have a boyfriend in Singapore. He is Indian. He makes 3,000 plus dollars. He helps me every month. He gives me gifts like phone and shoes . . . I never asked him for help. He knows my story. He says, 'Don't worry, I'll help you.' When we go out together, he never lets me spend. He has even given me 1,500 dollars to help me buy a house in the Philippines. I'm very thankful to this man.

Earlier, he used to be jealous and kept calling me non-stop on my off days to ask my whereabouts. Nowadays, I am with him the entire Sunday. I also keep my phone open to him so he has become okay. He talks to my family, and he can eat Filipino food. He likes my children and gives them birthday gifts. I also talk to his family but they're not very close to him, they talk only twice a month, on money matters.

People say that Indian people hold money tightly[24], because the Indians in the Philippines are like that. He's also like that—he buys me things but he will ask me not to buy anything unimportant, why waste money. He asks me to put my savings inside my bank account. He says things like why do you need makeup, soap is enough. Haha.

He plans to move to the Philippines, saying if we can save money in Singapore, then we can go to the Philippines and do business. I want to open a *sari-sari* store[25] in Cavite, where there is no flood. We want to buy my father a van so he can do delivery with it, instead of working for someone.

I'm seeing a future with my boyfriend . . . but I'm not banking on his help. I'm not taking it as a promise from him. Sometimes people just say things . . . we can't expect . . . if I expect and they don't give, then it will be so painful . . .

When I go back, I'll be stricter with my children. There're drugs around my place, and my children are boys . . . I need to be strict. I want them to study. I don't want them to be like other men in the Philippines, waiting for nothing . . . not liking any work . . . just like their father.

My younger one wants to become a policeman. The elder one wants to be a fireman. I want them to become seamen—good money, can enjoy life too.

If I could dream, I want to relax and travel abroad like rich people do. I want to go to the beach and party, wearing expensive things. I imagine myself sitting on a yacht in a swimsuit. I just want to have a drink with my friends . . . then we go to the salon, do our hair . . . I see that in the movies only (laughs). But I won't do Botox . . . people can die from such things . . .

I want to go to America. Maybe San Francisco . . . is it part of America? I want America, I don't know which part of America, but I want to go there. When I was young, they said I should go to America, because I was very dark and the white people would like my

---

[24] Stingy
[25] Neighbourhood grocery shop

beauty. I said maybe they'll throw me in the canyon or send me to Afghanistan. (laughs)

If I can go back in time, I want to go back to my childhood, I want to study. Then my life would have been better and I wouldn't have to work like this. I would choose nice courses like nursing, go abroad and make better money. Maybe I won't have children so early.

Before I die, I want to say one last thing to my family, 'Sorry mother . . . Sorry father. Sorry, my babies . . . Please forgive me. I needed to work overseas in order to support you. I love you, sorry for not being there on your birthdays, or Christmas. I am sorry . . . '

I Missed My Daughter's Biggest Day

H.D. Waruni Nimalka Perera (Sri Lanka), fifty-three years old, Domestic Worker in Singapore.

I was born in a village near Colombo. My father was a government employee in the Railways Department. I studied in a small and poor school. They taught us many subjects, but we had few books. Yet, I studied very hard and had good results at O-Level and A-Level exams. When my father passed away, I was about to stop schooling. Thanks to some teachers' help, I continued.

There was a shortage of teachers in Sri Lanka back then; there were hardly any in my village. So in my free time, I volunteered to teach preschool children basic English and Sinhalese. I remember the sad life of many children there. Nowadays whenever I visit my village, people there ask me to stay and start a school.

I also did other social work in the community. In Sri Lanka, it is common for couples to cohabit instead of marrying. It became an issue when their children reached school age because the schools required marriage certificates. I once organized a marriage ceremony for fifty such couples. They came so well-dressed. The government office issued marriage certificates for all of them. I was very happy.

But I didn't want to get married myself. I remained single for many years, even after all my younger siblings got married. This was because

I saw too many people with marital problems. Many Sri Lankan men were heavy drinkers. That causes problems.

At thirty, I wanted to become a nun in a Buddhist temple. My mother cried a lot, 'After I die, what will happen to you?' She didn't give me permission and found me a husband instead. I refused to marry him and left to work in Singapore.

My job in Singapore was to take care of an autistic boy in a Sri Lankan family. My employer liked my background as a teacher. They treated me well and I often travelled back to Sri Lanka with them.

After working in Singapore for six years, my mother found me a husband again. This time, I listened to her and got married. Just three weeks later, I returned to Singapore—I had promised my employer to come back. Besides, all my belongings were in Singapore. Two years later, my employer's family migrated to Australia. I returned to Sri Lanka to live with my husband. He turned out to be a bad man. He drank a lot and fought with me. I was sad and my family was also sad for me . . . Eventually, I left him and went to live with my mother. My husband and I never divorced but I told him that I couldn't be with him. I was very sad (sobs). I was pregnant with my daughter then.

I came back to Singapore when my daughter was only 1.5 years old (sobs). My sister looked after her and my mother. My baby was only 1.5 years old . . . My feeling was . . . (sobs)

This time, I worked for a North Indian family. There was a lot of work. I woke up at 4 a.m. in the morning and could only go to bed after midnight. My employer made me hand wash all clothes and even bedsheets. It was hard work. I had to iron all these daily but they let me do it only after I had finished all other work; that would be only after 10 p.m. By the time I was done, my daughter would have already gone to bed. For many days I never heard my baby's voice (sobs), because Ma'am didn't allow me to use the phone while working. This was the first time I was away from my girl. One morning I secretly called home to hear her voice and was caught by Ma'am. She asked me for my phone, but I refused to give it to her. After working there for two weeks, I requested for a change of employer.

The second employer was better. It was a Singaporean South Indian employer. My Ma'am was very kind. When she was angry, she would shout at me. But the next minute, she would cry, touch me, and say sorry. She was a very good person. I liked her so much. After working for her for six years, I decided to return to Sri Lanka. One day, after she had heard about my decision, my Ma'am came back from the market crying. When I opened the door, she hugged me. I thought that something had happened to Sir and started crying with her. Eventually, I asked her why she was crying. She said, 'When I boarded the bus, I realized that next month you will not be here anymore . . . how . . . I cried on the bus and couldn't go market . . . '

I went back to Sri Lanka because my daughter had started pre-school. I wanted to be there with her then. Her school was expensive so I worked in her school as a teacher to get her school fee waived. I also started a small food business. It was doing well, I had many customers. I was making a lot of money, sometimes one lakh Sri Lanka rupees a month. But I could only sleep for one or two hours a day. Moreover in Sri Lanka, I was living in my sister's house and I didn't want that. I wanted to build my own house. My ex-employer was also chasing me to return. My sister said, 'Why do you need to go back to Singapore? You have a business.' After ten months, I came back to Singapore.

When I went back home during my first year in Singapore, my daughter didn't know who I was . . . Those days she hadn't learned to talk but I still wanted to hear her voice . . . and then slowly she could call me, 'ah ma ah ma . . . '

My daughter is twelve years old now—she is a big girl. I visited her every year but since COVID-19, I couldn't go back. She complains that I don't want to see her. But I do video calls with her every day. In Sri Lanka, a girl's first period is a big day. The girl's mother needs to arrange everything for the ceremony, such as making herbal water for bathing. The father is supposed to give jewellery to the girl. Her big day was in December last year. That day I was very sad because I couldn't be there for her. And her father has never seen her . . . My daughter never asks about him. She calls my sister her mother and my sister's husband her father, even though she knows that I am her real mother.

I really want to be with my daughter. Next year, I want to go back and start my own business. I'll take many memories back to Sri Lanka. Half of my life has been in Singapore and I know many people here. In Sri Lanka, I don't even know Colombo enough; I can't even go around there without my sister's help.

When I go back to Sri Lanka, I will not marry again. When my daughter was still young, my family asked me to get divorced and marry someone else. My sister offered to take care of my daughter if that was to become an issue. But I have decided that I'd never marry again. I can't trust men; there are many rape cases of daughters by the (step)fathers, especially in Sri Lanka. So scary. I've never had boyfriends in Singapore. Sometimes, some Indian migrant workers ask for my number. I pretend as if I haven't heard anything; I just walk on.

With the money I earned in Singapore, I bought some land for my daughter. I am also building a house in Sri Lanka. My daughter says, 'We have enough money, Ma, you come.' I say, 'It's not enough; we don't have our own house yet, how?' She replies, 'I'll become a doctor and make money.' It will be so nice if she can be a doctor.

Dream for myself? I never thought about such things. My dream is to see my daughter finish her studies, get a job, and get married . . . then my life will be complete. I have always prepared her for the day when I'm no more, so that she will be able to take care of herself without needing anyone. Once my dreams for my daughter are fulfilled, I won't be sad if I die the very next day.

I Take Care of Other's Daughter and Mother—When Can I Take Care of My Own?

Joan Santilan (The Philippines), forty-one years old, Domestic Worker in Malaysia

I was born in Caloocan city in the Philippines. When I was ten, my parents broke up. Growing up with my mum and two younger siblings was tough. My mum was only a contract worker in a packaging company. My father did not support us much as he had another woman. I never had a school-bag; I just used plastic bags to keep my things. I didn't have proper shoes. I wore slippers with holes; they caused me to slip and fall on rainy days. I had only one piece of school uniform which I washed daily so it would be ready for the next day. I had to take care of my younger sister; she would sit with me the whole day in my classroom.

I wrote about my difficult childhood in an English-writing competition. I was only a third grader then, in primary school. I won the top prize even though many other participants were much older than me; some were even in college. The prize was a big volume of encyclopedia. I was so excited even though I didn't know how it could help me. Later, I learned that the prize was only an 80 per cent discount off the list price. My family couldn't afford the remaining twenty per cent so I didn't get my prize. But because of this, I felt very proud of myself throughout my school years. The organizers said that I deserved a bright future. 'My daughter won the competition!' Even today my mother boasts to everyone.

My grandfather, an air force veteran, was also an artistic person. He carved, he painted; all his paintings were donated to a church after his death. He liked to read. He gave me books as birthday gifts. Those books were too heavy for me to understand. But I loved the pictures, especially those black and white ones of buildings and architecture. My grandfather told me about building structures and styles. Because of his influence, I dreamed of becoming a Civil Engineer. I wanted to build buildings that could last a hundred years. As a child, my mind was filled with numbers: weights, heights. When I saw a nice and strong house, the mind became busy calculating the number of bags of cement and the number of pillars needed to build something like that . . .

These thoughts of building houses also bring back very tragic childhood memories. We lived near a river. During a strong typhoon, the flood broke the dam and swept away our house. We had nothing left except for the clothes upon us. My mum was crying, not because our house was gone, but for our animals: our dogs, cats and chickens . . . they were all washed away. My mum and I built our house again. We found a saw. We bought nails. With bamboo, we made our wardrobe, flooring, and walls. We made a tin roof . . . Nobody had taught us anything.

When I was 16, I dropped out of school. I really wished to attend high school, but I had to help my mum. I took up work in a gasoline station. I started there as a cashier and was later promoted to be the manager-in-charge. A teacher offered to help me continue with my studies. During lunch break, I skipped food, rode a motorbike to her place and got tuition from her. I did this every day for three months. I graduated with the highest scores in my school. I didn't go to college though. I thought that for someone like me, high school education was more than enough. But if one day I am given the chance to go to college without having to worry about money, I would definitely say yes.

Along the way, I fell in love somehow. He was a very popular guy who had many friends, boys and girls . . . My mother told me 'No'. She didn't trust him. She said that he would cheat on me. Even my sister-in-law, who was also my best friend, said, 'Don't marry my brother. He will not take care of you.' They were both right. I was eighteen when I became pregnant. He was twenty-one. We got married the next year. Since young, I had been living in a cage, having to support my mother and siblings . . . I saw marriage as the way out. It was my way to rebel against my situation. But we were not mature enough to handle family life.

My second daughter was barely a year old when my husband started seeing another woman. We separated. It was a very difficult time because besides taking care of my children, I still had to help my mother and siblings. But I didn't ask my husband for any support. I just pushed myself and chose to migrate, to work as a domestic helper in Malaysia.

To migrate was not an easy decision; my younger daughter being just one year old then . . . I asked God if I should go to Malaysia and then I had a dream that I will never forget. In that dream I saw myself as a butterfly, freely crossing a river. In my own interpretation, it was a sign that God gave me permission. That's why I love butterflies. I feel that they love me too. When I stretch out my hands, they land on them and stay. It's so divine.

In Malaysia, my job was to take care of a two-year-old girl in addition to cleaning the whole house; all three floors, a patio, and a car, besides doing laundry, showering a dog, ironing clothes, and watering plants among other household chores. My good time management skills were helpful.

Most of the time, I was with my employer's parents: the *Ah Ma*[26] and the *Gong Gong*[27]. Once I asked Ah Ma for toothpaste because at that time, I was not allowed to go out myself. Ah Ma didn't speak English and I didn't know how to say the word 'Toothpaste' in Malay or Chinese. So, I told her that I wanted a 'Colgate'. This became a big

---

[26] Grandmother
[27] Grandfather

issue. Ah Ma complained to my lady boss that I was so choosy that I wanted a Colgate[28]. My lady boss scolded me in front of everyone, questioning why I was so '*mei you li mao*'[29]. I cried, saying, 'I don't want to argue, if you don't want to buy toothpaste for me, then so be it . . . ' Ah Ma started disliking me after this incident.

I worked hard to improve their perception of me, to gain their trust and respect. I tried to learn about Ah Ma's likes, needs, wants, and her ways of thinking. I cared for her with love, as if she was my own grandmother. It was worth it. I have been with the same employer ever since I came to Malaysia. They treat me like family now.

At their family gatherings during Chinese New Year, I am seated with them, at the same dining table. They ask me to taste all their food. Gong Gong introduces me to relatives and friends as their own child. Gong Gong is so similar to my own grandfather. We share the same love for arts and crafts. He does Chinese calligraphy. Together we have made some monkey pots[30]. Gong Gong said to me, 'You are special, that's why you stay here for so long. We love you. And we don't want you to go . . . ' Oh this makes me cry! (tears)

In my first year in Malaysia, it was hard for me to tolerate the spicy local food. My Ma'am used to make a separate non-spicy portion just for me. Gong Gong also cooked a non-spicy version of Nasi Lemak[31] which I fell in love with. Slowly I began to like the food here, like fish head curry, goat curry, all vegetable curry dishes, and most of all, laksa. Of course, I still miss our food from the Philippines, pork adobo, sinigan bamos, sour soup . . . oh how I miss them . . . I cannot cook our food here except for pork adobo for my little buddy. She calls it 'the Filipino pork'.

11 November 2021 marks my eleventh year in Malaysia. I'm happier now. I don't think too much. I feel more peaceful. I have become more broad-minded and observant. I understand that people have their own issues. For example, when Ma'am brings her work

---

[28] Colgate-branded toothpaste
[29] Means 'no manners' in Chinese
[30] Decorative item made of fruit shells
[31] Coconut Rice

issues home and becomes hot tempered, I don't talk much and just listen. When I get a long message from her, I analyse the message and just reply, 'Okay Ma'am, don't worry'. But I'm also more cautious now. I don't simply trust people, especially on the internet. There are many friend invitations that I have not accepted. On my last day on earth, I will close all my social accounts.

I'm happy living by myself. I sing all the time. If my Ma'am doesn't hear my singing, she gets worried that something is wrong. Now I run a small business on Facebook selling necklaces. I have the blessings from my employer. The necklaces are made of natural healing stones. My favourite stone is lapis lazuli, a blue stone that boosts calmness and focus. I use gold dust to create a classic and elegant look in my necklaces. I draw. On paper and canvas, I sketch people, motivational quotes, or anything that comes into my mind like 'Zing!' I'm a free soul. My mind is always on another dimension. 'What colour should I put on my painting?' This makes me smile even when I'm cleaning the toilet bowl.

My husband passed away a few years ago. Just a month before he died, he apologized for everything and asked to rescue our marriage. I was touched . . . but I said, 'I don't want to destroy another family.' I had forgiven him and his mistress long ago. But I just cannot forget what he said just a month before his death, that he still loved me.

I returned to the Philippines to attend the funeral. His mistress was still acting a little competitive; she thinks my late husband loved her more, her six children with him being her evidence. It's okay. I am not interested in any competition to have more children. I went to the government office to waive my rights as the legal wife so that all my benefits could go to his mistress. I only took the part that belonged to my children. The lady officer asked, 'Why?' But seeing her children caught in this life situation—the youngest still a baby—broke my heart. If I were in her situation, I'd have surely taken my own life. I feel a lot more blessed because I have work. I could send my children to school, pay for my mum's medication, and even help my brother and sister . . . I indeed received more than I could wish for, didn't I?

Many people ask me to find love again. My mum warns that I'd be left alone when my girls leave home. My sister-in-law asks me to marry someone in Malaysia. But I cannot force love. I say to them, 'If it's time, it's time.' Mr Right hasn't found the right way to me yet. I don't want another stone to hit me on my head.

I'm not into handsome looks. I just want a handsome heart, someone who accepts my children and my past, supports me in whatever I want to do, someone who loves, cares for, and respects me. I don't need his money—I can provide for myself. Maybe this is why I can't find that 'someone.' My mother thinks that men are overpowered by me and that I need to lower my confidence. But I tell her that men will take advantage of me if I am not this confident. A lot of such things happen on social media. Men meet women and tell them 'I love you'. The weaker women will fall for them.

For me, being a widow is a blessing. My late husband made me the strong person I am today. My imperfect life and marriage, everything in my past, has strengthened me. They have made me grow as a woman. I love who I am right now.

My boss's baby has now become a young lady . . . and my best friend . . . My little friend calls me all kinds of names like princess, bear, Kata . . . When back from school, she starts calling me from right outside the house like 'Princess! Princess!' She's thirteen now, my younger girl is twelve. My little friend sends her old clothes to my younger one. They are friends on Facebook. It feels nice.

I see my younger self in my younger daughter. While she is good at studies, she's also into arts like drawing and poetry performance. She has a small corner in the house that serves as an art gallery for her own work. She loves to show me her latest art during our video calls. I've been saving up for her college. I want to support her education as far as she can go. Given her heart to help people, maybe she will become a good nurse. I never forced my daughters to study hard. But I'm very strict with my younger one when it comes to mathematics. I'll make sure that she has completed her math homework to her best ability. During our video calls, I don't simply give her the answers. Instead, I give her clues for the more difficult problems. I ask her, 'Are you asking me the answer or the way to answer the question?'

My eldest daughter is twenty-two. She got married last June but the wedding party couldn't happen because of COVID. She has struggled and suffered a lot because of my absence. She had to look after her younger sister. My salary was only 800 ringgit, not enough for all the monthly expenses; milk, diaper, school supplies, and electricity . . . But my eldest daughter persevered through all these. She is strong like me. She has a one-year-old baby now. But she still takes care of her younger sister on my behalf.

My mum has always been my best support. She took care of both of my daughters, and now my granddaughter also stays with her. She's getting old. She has had a stroke twice; half of her body is paralysed. She says, 'You come back for good and take care of your own girls now.' But if I go back, we will all suffer. It's very hard to find a job in the Philippines.

Even otherwise, I will find it hard to go back . . . I have such a strong connection with my little buddy, as if she is my own. I think she listens to me more than her own mum. I'm strict with her. I teach her to be independent, to protect and take care of herself. For example, I teach her the right way to wash her panties and keep them away from others. She is going through puberty. It's necessary for somebody to be with her through this phase. Her mother is always at work. She doesn't talk to her grandparents. She will have no one if I leave.

I feel torn between two huge rocks pulling me apart . . . a part of my heart is here . . . the other part of my heart is with my family. I'm not getting any younger, neither is my mum. I have been taking care of other people's kids, their mom . . . When will God allow me to go back home, so that I can take care of my own kids and my own mum? I'm still praying for the signal.

Sacrifice, I Sacrifice, for Everyone in My Life

Elpidia Abel Malicsi (The Philippines), sixty-four years old, Domestic Worker, worked in Saudi Arabia, currently working in Hong Kong

I was the second youngest child in my family. Because of my unusually dark skin, I used to ask my father if I was his daughter.

I grew up being very religious and wanted to become a nun after I finished high school. My mother didn't like the idea, so I ran away from my family. But later I changed my mind and started working in a store. A niece told me that a teacher was looking for a helper. With her referral, I got the job. This teacher also helped me with my studies. This was how I went to university and graduated in 1980 with a major in Secretarial Studies. When we are determined to sacrifice, we can achieve anything.

As there were no good jobs in the Philippines, I went to Saudi in 1989 to work as a domestic worker. It was very tough there. As the only helper in the house, I took care of four children and thirteen rooms. Most days, I could sleep only from 1 a.m. to 5 a.m. The most difficult part was not being able to shower, especially during my periods. They didn't have a culture of taking showers. But I sacrificed. I persevered.

Within three months, I learned to speak Arabic and cook their recipes. During Ramadan, I fasted with my employer's family for the whole month. Sacrifice, I sacrifice.

After working with this family for four years, I found another employer who took me to Germany for six months. When they were about to move again, this time to the USA, I said no. My mother was getting old and I wanted to stay closer to her in case something happened. I found work in Hong Kong. Two years later, I got married in the Philippines. I gave birth to our little girl a few years later.

When my daughter was two, I went back to Hong Kong. I've been working with the same employer since then; it has been twenty-one years. When I was diagnosed with breast cancer in 2013, my niece also joined me to work in this family. My employer took good care of me and I have since recovered. My niece and I live in the same room and share a bunk bed.

I have looked after my employer's daughter since she was young. I was so happy to have successfully trained the then three-month-old baby to sleep alone in her room. Today she's like my own; she talks to me about all her problems . . . I'm so happy about it.

I'm also very close to my own daughter, but it's a little different because I was never a caregiver for her. Sometimes she says things that I don't like. My husband says that I have been staying in Hong Kong for so long because I love my 'daughter' there. Living away from my own child and husband is a sacrifice I made in order to support my family. All these years, I saved up for my daughter's university education. She has started working now. I have also supported a niece and a nephew to finish their university. My income also gave my mother a good life. All this is fulfilling. I have no regrets for making such a sacrifice.

When I go back to the Philippines, I want to run my own business, something related to designing things. I am a self-made designer. Some of the gowns I made with coffee sachets and painted bottles were exhibited in Hong Kong. I also make many other things like fruit-carvings. Since I was young, I liked painting and designing things. My mother was a tailor back then. I was too small to use her sewing machine, but I learned to sew by hand and could make any dress I wanted.

Some years back, my husband had a stroke; half of his body is paralysed although he can manage himself. Do I have any dreams left? My only dream is to I just want to take my poor husband and my daughter for a holiday, just to be all together by the sea side.

Maybe I'm Obsessed,
But My Children are My Life

Erin Cipta (Indonesia), forty-three years old, Business Owner,
former Domestic Worker in Taiwan

I was born in a small village in Java, Indonesia. My parents were *Wayang*[32] artists. We were poor—we didn't even have electricity—but we were happy. My seven siblings and I filled our house with screams of laughter.

I studied till high school in an Islamic boarding school in the city. There, I became more social. I took literature classes, joined a writing club, and even got some of my works published in magazines and newspapers. Unfortunately, my parents had difficulty supporting my education after high school. As their fifth child, I was the so-called 'sandwich generation' who are asked to work and support the younger siblings. I should have fought for my own education; my life would have been very different . . . But back then, I lacked confidence; a primary school teacher had once said that I was stupid because I couldn't solve some math problem. So I didn't object to dropping out believing that my brothers were smarter than me.

---

[32] Javanese traditional theatre with puppets

I worked in shops until I had an arranged marriage at the age of twenty-eight. My husband and I started a business selling fertilizer and seeds. The business failed and we got heavily into debt.

I decided to work in Taiwan to pay off our debt. I left behind our two children; the elder one was four years old and the younger one was only two, still being breastfed. I was so sad . . . but it's over now . . . (sobs) I don't know . . . every time I remember this, I just feel awful but it's . . . it's over . . . (sobs)

I worked as a helper and a house nurse for an elderly couple in Taipei. My main job was to take care of Ah Gong[33], a heart patient. The Ah Ma[34] ran their company and was in the office on weekdays. They were nice to me. I was not used to the fast-paced life in Taiwan but Ah Ma guided me patiently; I spoke no Mandarin so they spoke in English with me. When I didn't have the money to buy my a phone, they lent me their phone to call my family; knowing my religion, they set me up a place to pray near the laundry area and allowed me to wear headscarf outside. I knew I was lucky—not every helper has such employers.

Yet, the first year was not easy. In my contract, I agreed to get extra pay instead of having off-days. After all, I was not there to explore the beauty of Taiwan but to work and solve my financial problems. Still, it was very hard to have no off-day for three years I was very bored and sometimes needed a break badly.

Ah Ma and Ah Gong often complained about my absent-mindedness. They were right. I couldn't work with the whole me. My body, my hands, and my legs were working, but my heart was missing. I couldn't hold my longing for my children (sobs). I often cried at night. Once, both my children got sick. Even though my mother-in-law took very good care of them, I cried non-stop, feeling like a bad mother . . . (sobs) because I couldn't be with them when they needed me the most . . . Ah Ma said, 'You have to be patient because we need you here also. Just pray.' What could I do? I couldn't step back. I had to finish what I had started.

---

[33] Grandpa
[34] Grandma

Things became more difficult whenever Ah Gong fell sick. I had to be with him in the hospital. Sometimes I only slept for three or four hours a day and this would continue for weeks. Although Ah Ma fed me very good food—vegetables, fruits, and occasionally Indonesian meat and fish dishes—I was just too tired. I became very thin.

When Ah Gong was better, the work was more manageable. At night, I could rest in my own room. But even then, the challenging part was Ah Gong's 'obsessiveness' with me (laughs): He wanted me to be around him all the time. If I was away for a moment, he would call. For the whole day, I had no privacy and couldn't do anything for myself. I couldn't even look at my mobile phone because Ah Gong didn't like it.

In Taiwan, I had limited interactions with other locals. But I still remember how some Taiwanese saw us as lower creatures. Once, when I took care of Ah Gong in the hospital, a patient in the same ward said, 'This girl is so thin, how can she take care of Ah Gong? And the Indonesians are so stupid.' Grocers scolded me because I couldn't speak Mandarin well. They said, 'Why are you so confused? Why are you *hen ben*[35]?' I was so traumatized to go to markets. To avoid talking, I would ask Ah Ma for shopping lists written in Chinese.

I worked until the last day of my contract and went back to Indonesia in July 2015. Ah Gong and Ah Ma gave me many presents including a bicycle for my children and a jade necklace for me. I still wear it. At that time, Ah Gong was almost ninety, and Ah Ma had just celebrated her seventy-one-year birthday. She was still very healthy. After plastic surgery in Korea, she looked as beautiful as a young lady. But she was very forgetful. When she forgot things at home, she would come back and scream, 'Give me this thing . . . ' Her panic made me laugh a lot. I'm still in touch with Ah Ma. She sends me pictures of her grandchildren. It feels nice.

I worked in Taiwan for three years. Within the first year, we cleared our debt completely. In the second and the third year, we built some savings for the rest of our lives. We also bought back the paddy field we had lost earlier.

---

[35] Very dim wit

Now we plant rice in our fields. I also get some income from a traditional drinks business and my writing. My recent book is about the friendship between a dog and a Taiwanese boy with Down syndrome. I want to tell people that every child is special, and that handicapped children can live normally like others. I also write about sexual abuse and child marriage in Indonesia. In Taiwan, I read about people campaigning on these issues and became aware of them. I'm writing now to increase awareness in my own country.

Inspired by the Brilliant Times bookstore in Taipei, I started a library in my village. It was initially meant for mothers but now it is for everyone, especially the children of my village. I have been collecting children's books because the children are so curious. We closed the library last year because of COVID-19 rules but now we are reopening.

Ah Gong and Ah Ma said that I could work for them again if I wanted. But I have decided to come home for good. I know I can earn more if I work in Taiwan, but no longer can I stand being away from my children. I think I made the right decision. Now I'm happy seeing them growing well, doing well in school . . . The younger one wants to become a policewoman . . . (laughs). Whatever they want to be, I will support them.

Maybe I'm obsessed, but they are my life.

Abba, I Want to Come Back

Sagar (Bangladesh), thirty-five years old,
Construction Worker in Singapore

I come from Tangail, Bangladesh. I am the second among my parents' three sons. My father used to work in the police and my mother is a homemaker.

My father tried hard to get me a job in England. He thought I could work in a hotel there. He was well connected to many important people in Bangladesh. He thought they could help me. This was during the Khaleda Zia government in Bangladesh. Suddenly, her government fell. All the important people my father knew became unimportant. Going to England was no longer possible. My father asked me to try to join the army instead. But I didn't want to be a soldier. I had a friend who was working in Singapore; his brother was an agent who brought people from Bangladesh to Singapore. They asked me to come to Singapore as a migrant worker. My friend's brother took 50,000 taka from me. Then he disappeared.

I had already been through an institute in Dhaka that trained aspiring migrant workers for Singapore. So I thought of still trying to make it to Singapore. But where could I get the extra money? So I asked my father to retire because when one retires from a government job in Bangladesh, he can get some lump sum money. My father retired in 2008 and I came over to Singapore.

For my first few days in Singapore, the agency put me in a small room on top of a disco, along with five other migrant workers. It was impossible to sleep at night because of all the noise. We had very little to eat as well. We kept calling the agency for food and eventually someone would come after a long time to bring us some.

After a few days, they took us to the work site. It was a construction site. I had never seen anything like this before. They immediately put me on heavy work. I had to cut heavy iron rods and move them around. I felt very sad. I didn't want to do such work. I felt so disheartened. I called home that very night and I told my father, 'Abba, I want to come back'.

My father said that they have spent so much money to send me to Singapore. He had even retired for my sake. So I must stay put. He said that everyone in the family was looking at me to support the household. So I must keep on working. I kept on working.

My company put me together with a Chinese worker. He was a lot more experienced. He helped me a lot. He told me, 'I will cut the rods for you; just whenever the supervisor comes, you pretend that you are the one cutting.' Slowly, with his help, I learned the work. But I still made mistakes now and then. People were so rude then. So after one year I again told my parents that I wanted to go back. But everyone in the family said, 'You made your father retire and we spent so much money to send you and we also had to take loans because of you; so you have to work.' That's how one year passed and then two years and now I have been in Singapore for more than thirteen years.

My saddest day in Singapore is also because of Chinese workers. One day I was lifting very heavy blocks of concrete. I was rather fat at that time so they gave me the job of moving heavy things. One of the blocks fell on my leg. I felt such pain! A few Chinese workers were standing nearby. They did nothing to help me. They just stood there laughing.

One day I had a big accident. An excavator ran over my leg. I was in so much pain. People just surrounded me but no one helped. Somebody said take him to the police. Somebody said take him to the doctor. Then an Indian man came. He just rubbed my head and said everything will be okay. Finally they took me to the hospital. They checked everything and then said that there was no problem. But I was bleeding. So much pain. Then they took me to another hospital. They said my leg was broken. I had surgery. After that they put me back in the dormitory. Two guards stood outside my room. For many days I couldn't move. I didn't know what was happening. My supervisor—he was a Bangladeshi as well—told me that he heard they were planning to send me back to Bangladesh. He said that I should actually talk to a lawyer, and then maybe I can get some compensation. So one day, I gave five dollars to one of the guards and I told him that I just needed to go to the doctor and come back. Instead I ran away and went to one lawyer. Because I had no money, I also approached an NGO called TWC2 who provided free food to migrant workers who were having problems. Once my case was settled, I got only two points. That money was just enough to pay one of the many loans that I had taken to come to Singapore.

Now I work for a different employer in Singapore. But things have not improved. My father has been sick. They have to take him to the doctor every week. He has some heart problems but the doctor thinks that he has cancer as well. Also our house in Bangladesh got swept away in the flood. So now they don't even have their own place anymore. They have to stay at my grandfather's place. The money I need to send back home keeps on increasing. And they keep saying, 'We only have your income to rely on, if you don't send us money all of us will go hungry.' So this is how my life is now. What can I do?

One day, my father called and said, 'You have to send me a lot of money; you have to send it immediately.' I was very surprised. He didn't give any reason about this urgent demand. I told him, 'I have no money, I have no savings. Whatever I earn, I send everything to you. How can I get you so much money all of a sudden?' Still I asked some friends and somehow managed to send the money to Bangladesh that very day. That evening I kept getting calls from Bangladesh. I couldn't talk then but after I finished my work, I called my father. He told me that my mother was dead. That very night, at 3 a.m., I went to Bangladesh, buried my mother, and came back.

My elder brother went to work in Saudi Arabia. He came back within one year and then he got married and he has children now. He has no income. He relies on my income. And my younger brother is now entering college. Who will pay for the fees? Moreover it is very hard to get a job in Bangladesh. If you want a government job you have to pay a lot of money. So there is not much hope for him either. So the whole family keeps relying on me for money. My life is over.

But at the end of a hard day's work, I think of all those faces back home. I am having a hard time but at least they can smile. They can have a good life. That is all that I care for.

I am thirty-five years old now. I couldn't marry. I couldn't start a family. My life is over. My friends make a lot of fun of me. They keep saying, 'Hey old man! You can get married to our children.' What can I do? My life is over. I have no hope.

I have a lot of nice ideas about starting new businesses. But Singapore will only think of me as a migrant worker. There is no future for my ideas. My life has no hope. You can see that I almost went to England and just then the Bangladesh government changed. So I am 100 per cent sure now that fate is against me. My life is over.

Part IV

Migrant workers come with many hopes and aspirations. But they can be taking huge risks. When things go wrong, they can go very wrong: some lose their lives or limbs due to accidents; some lose all their savings; some are abducted and sold as sex slaves. What happens when 'luck' is not on their side?

In this section, the featured migrant workers—Lalita Vadia and Durga Balan (India); Ataur Rahman, Mehedi Hassan, Mamun (Bangladesh); a group of homeless migrant workers from India; and a group of tea plantation workers from India—dwell on these questions and more as they narrate their life stories.

A Lifetime Under a Flyover

The homeless migrant workers in Mumbai, India

In Mumbai, there are slums, and then there are slums, and then there are the homeless, a word that seems too benign for their condition. Under the broad flyover, connecting Chembur with Ghatkopar, is one such settlement. These 'homes' for about twenty people is an uneven ground strewn with pebbles, scattered with chicken feathers and trash. One family has a tattered mattress for a bed. The others are just using old plastic sheets. Their belongings are meagre, all wrapped up in three cloth bundles. A young couple has dug in four poles around their sheets and hung old sarees around them to get some privacy. The traffic is blaring deafening horns from all directions. The air is full of dust and the smell of rot.

Rati, Shanti, Anant, Lalita, Nakul and others:

Last night . . . they came in a taxi . . . they tried to drag out our daughter . . . We beat them and then they ran away. See, we filed the police report, is it correct?

   'This is quite common,' says Shashikant Bhalerao, a social worker with Alternative Realities. 'Sometimes, strangers lie down next to a sleeping couple and try to fondle the wife. Sometimes, they are gang raped. When women are having shower, people will come and surround them and keep on looking. Sometimes, strangers come and throw stones on sleeping women.'

Rati, an elderly woman:

I have been homeless for more than forty years. I have seen my husband die here; four of my children died here. One of my little girls, I saw her get flattened by a truck with my own eyes, right here. We buried her near that pillar (sobs).

Anant, a man in his forties or fifties:

We are five families settled under this section of the flyover. We are all related to one another but came here separately, in different years. We are from Sholapur, a seven hours bus ride from Mumbai. On the other side of the pillars you see, there is another set of families. They are also from Maharashtra, some other village. We settle around wherever we can find jobs. This place is near that restaurant you see. They give us their leftover food everyday so we stay here.

Why do we need a house? I came here as a child and have no memory of any house. So I don't know if a house is better than here. From what I know about the cost of a house, not even ten generations of us, if they come together, can build one. But here, everything is free.

Look at my fingers. (They are all bloodied from old wounds.) I get them from pulling ropes to carry baskets full of chicken over my head.

We men do day jobs pasting Bollywood posters, digging roads, fixing gutters, cleaning streets, selling books[36] at traffic signals; whatever we can find on that day. Many days I don't get any work. On a good day, I can get 200 rupees. Some days, I just get fifty. The women, if they don't need to take care of the children, work as domestic helpers. Some make baskets, charms, brooms, anything they can make and sell in the traffic junctions, when the traffic light is red.

Shanti, a middle aged woman:

Most of us have been around for more than twenty years. Many came when very young. We keep moving. When the government will throw

---

[36] These are mostly pirated books

us away from here, we will have to move again. We had no land back in Sholapur. How could we have survived there?

My sister got married to one of the men here. They just went to the temple, got married, and came back. Among us, every family has to do their own cooking. We buy firewood. When it rains, we just move our sheets and the mattress to the spot where there is no water. But we fall sick during the rains. That family lost one child last year because of Tuberculosis. That baby, there, has got jaundice now.

The mother of the boy with jaundice, perhaps a teenager:

No, I didn't go to the doctor. I just got this charm from a priest; he asked me to put this as a necklace on the baby.

Nakul, a boy of five or six:

I don't go to school. There is so much work. During the day, I have to wash all the dishes and also bring water.

Nakul's mother, perhaps a teenager:

I want them to study and get out of here. But sometimes, I have to send them to ask for money from people stuck in traffic.

Lalita, a teenage girl:

See those trucks? They park these trucks here every night. These deliver chickens during the day. It is so smelly at night. See all these feathers here. There are many rats too. Some young babies had their fingers bitten off by the rats . . .

Please sit down. Here, have some tea . . .

You are holding your finished cup of tea as if it is such a precious thing. You can throw it anywhere. There is so much trash around anyway.

They Said There was a Better Job, But They Sold me as a Bride

Lalita Vadia (India), late-twenties, activist, former domestic migrant worker in India

I was born in a field, in Ratanpur Panchayat[37] area, part of Betul district of Madhya Pradesh. We were so poor that we didn't even have a house. We lived in the field till a government programme gave us a house. My father was a servant to a moneylender. Our parents worked as hired hands. We were five siblings but one boy died in a tractor accident.

I have been working alongside my parents as a day labourer since I was twelve years old, for 10 rupees a day. I didn't have any schooling. But we were a happy family. There was enough to eat. I had many friends. We used to play *kabaddi*, celebrate festivals like Holi, pool in money to have a picnic on New Year's Day. I had a happy childhood.

When I was twenty-three, a woman from our village called Rajni said that she would find us jobs in a 'company'. This was the time of the year when there was no work in the sugarcane fields. We were all short of money. Rajni said that it was a good job; we would be sitting

---

[37] A panchayat is the smallest administrative subdivision in India, typically representing a village

'inside an office'.[38] We took her offer. I left our village together with my mother, my younger brother, our neighbour and a few others.

Rajni brought us to the big city of Pune. Once there, we realized that there was no 'company'. It was a construction job. I had to carry bricks and sand, up and down the many levels being built. I had never done such work before. We were kept in a slum. Our house was just a cloth hung over four poles.

After working for a few days, Rajni came to my mother and asked if she could take me with her for a better job. She then put me on a train. I was surprised. I asked why we needed to take the train. She said we were going to the work-site. Since I was illiterate, I didn't even know where the train was going.

We got down at Mandideep. I was sick by then, cold and coughing. We stayed there for two days and then Rajni said, 'Let's go to Bhopal and show you to a doctor'. I pleaded with her to put me on a train back home. She declined saying all will be fine At Bhopal, I wasn't taken to any doctor. Instead she said, 'Let's go to this nearby town of Shajapur.' I was very sick and weak by then. I couldn't even stand. She called someone on the phone. Two men came in an auto-rickshaw and forced me inside. One of them slapped me. On the way to Shajapur, I heard Rajni telling the men that I was a tribal girl, a Gond.

At Shajapur, they locked me up in a room. I was crying. Next day, a few groups of people came to see me. They would come in, have a look at me, and then go away. I was sold to one of the groups. At night, they came to take me to their village. They beat me when I protested.

At the village, they took me to a house. There I was introduced to a boy named Ravi. I was so perplexed by what was happening. They called my relatives to get my identity number details. While they talked, they put a knife to my throat so that I would stay quiet.

The next day, they took me to a court and forced me to sign some documents. Then, they said that I was now married to this Ravi. I was so confused. All along, they were threatening to beat me. They forced me to smile and pose for pictures with him. I saw Ravi's family

---

[38] Implies work that doesn't involve toiling in the hot sun

pay 55,000 rupees to the three who had kidnapped me; Rajni, Bansi Gujjar and Dule Singh Gujjar. As they left, I ran after them. The boy I was allegedly married to, grabbed me, and forced me back into their house.

I was locked up in one room. I was not allowed to go out even once. Outside the room, the boy's parents stood guard all the time. Sometimes the boy would come inside . . . I would scream wildly. Then they would beat me with wooden planks. At times, they would enact a mock hanging on me, putting a noose on my neck and tying it to the fan. Sometimes, they put heavy bags of sand on my head. They would turn on a recorder and ask me to say that I got married out of my own will. I said that they could kill me if they wanted but I would never say that.

My parents didn't even know that I had been sold. Much later, someone told my papa about my real situation. My papa was sick at that time. After he recovered, my parents went to the police station. The police summoned Rajni who told everyone that I was six months pregnant and there was no point bringing me back. My parents then approached Jan Sahas[39]. The NGO helped them a lot. After knocking on the police door for many days and many more struggles, I was eventually rescued on 9 January 2018.

Those six months of being taken hostage were like six years for me. There was not a single day that I didn't cry. I thought of my home every moment. I thought of committing suicide but I was certain that my papa would come for me. That hope is what helped me to survive.

I caught tuberculosis in that house. I have not fully recovered yet; I still keep coughing. Even after I was free, I was insulted so many times by so many people. They would say, 'Girls like you have such fate only,' or 'You girls from Betul are just like this.' Earlier the people of my village would say, 'She was such a good girl, this shouldn't have happened to her.' Now the same people say, 'Why did you bring her back to our village? We don't want her.' They insult my father. They don't invite our family for weddings. When I go to fetch water, they

---

[39] An NGO that works with migrant communities

cover their faces if they see me, spit on the road, and wash the tap thoroughly once I am gone. Even my friends have abandoned me. Because of all this, my beloved papa has changed. He fights with me all the time. He picks on me for small things. Once he even took an axe to kill me. When outsiders say something, I ignore it. But when someone from my family says something, I lose my will to live.

I have now joined Jan Sahas, the NGO, as a volunteer. There, I have learnt to read. I can write a little as well. I joined many of their programs like helplines for migrant workers. I tell migrant workers about their constitutional rights. I participated extensively in *Garima Yatra*.[40]

As a child, I was so scared of the police. Whenever I saw them, I would run away. But since my incident, I have spent so much time with them. At first, I couldn't say anything to the police. I would cry all the time. But now, I have become stronger. I have given up thoughts of suicide. I speak up to my father as well. I am no longer scared of travelling alone. I have since been to many parts of India as part of my work with Jan Sahas. I know how to buy my own tickets. I know which train to board. I have learnt so many new things.

While working for Jan Sahas, I have come to know of the many challenges faced by migrant workers. During the first COVID lockdown, there were no jobs. But all prices went up; cooking oil that cost 100 rupees was now 200. Migrant workers and their families had nothing to eat. By begging and borrowing, they survived. Now, some have begun working again. But many don't get paid. They don't even have any pay slips. Their families keep calling them, 'What happened, send us money, what will we eat?' The migrant worker gives up and eventually goes back home, foregoing their due pay.

So many female migrant workers are missing, just like I was. They left their home on the promise of a good 'company' job, but no one knows what happened to them. Their families don't even know the whereabouts of the middlemen who took them away. These things happen a lot more with *Adivasis*[41] like us who are less educated and poorer.

---

[40] Dignity March - held across India by women who are survivors of sexual violence
[41] A word for aboriginal tribal people in India

Going forward, I want to set up a platform to help poor people understand and obtain their constitutional rights, like their right to education. Poor families like mine—out of financial constraints—stop sending their kids to school. Our children also then end up as labourers. There is no improvement across generations. If we are educated, we can be exploited less. No girl should have to go through what I had to. That's my only wish.

It is a common practice in India for the middlemen to visit villages promising work. They come knowing when the villagers are in dire need of money, just before the agricultural season, or before a wedding. These middlemen have their agents in the villages so they know which family is in what situation and specifically target the vulnerable ones. They make false promises. They say the women will get a good 'company' job. They will deposit a big amount, 30,000 or 50,000 rupees saying this is an advance salary for six months or one year of work. But most women end up in low paying jobs such as working as a 24*7 maid. Their families have no clue. The men end up working in brick plants or construction jobs Often, they are cheated of their due wages.

Sumit Singh, Jan Sahas

Everyone Wants to Leave but There is Nothing Better Outside

Tea Plantation Workers (Baganias) in Assam, India

The state of Assam is arguably the most diverse of places in the already uber-diverse region of North-east India. Over hundreds of years, people of Dravidian, Mongoloid, or Caucasian origins have migrated here, creating an entangled history that has turned Assam into a battlefield for every possible—if competing—human claim.

In the early nineteenth century, the British colonists brought in to Assam, workers from the tribal belts of eastern, southern and central India in large numbers for the commercial cultivation of the famed Assam tea. Today, the six million Bagania—tea plantation workers and their families—constitute more than a fifth of Assam's population.

The workers were housed by the British in settlements called Lines, rows of shacks alongside the tea garden, with shared communal facilities. With its system of exploitative recruitment agents and middlemen, brutal working and living conditions characterized by frequent physical assaults, and an inability to escape from this form of indentured labor, the situation of the tea tribes bore stark resemblance to that of the slaves deployed in cotton plantations in the American South. Life has barely changed for the better in the Lines of Assam since then.

At one such Line at Baxung near Jorhat, the beauty of the tamed nature can be mesmerizing. The tea plantations present a horizon flooded with a frozen sea of green, held back in time by tall shade trees piercing through them. There, we met a group of eight female workers. Half of them were perhaps in their thirties; the rest could have been teenagers. Their skin was dark, their bodies lean. Their faces were bony and the tallest among them was perhaps less than five feet. All wore brightly coloured sarees. One of them spoke to us about life in Baxung. She spoke in Bagania language[42] that was translated for us by Rao.

Lai (name changed), perhaps in her thirties:

Babu![43] What's there to know about our lives? Every day, we work from seven in the morning till four in the evening. I have been working like this for fifteen years or twenty, I don't remember. I was not born here, but in another tea estate. I came here after I got married. I live in that house, you see. Our houses are in the same cluster.

My husband also works here, but he is with other people. Men do different things like cutting, grafting, and spraying chemicals. Their job is much harder. We women do the plucking of the tea leaves.

They pay us 200 rupees for a day but during peak plucking season in August or September, they pay us by weight. Now, during winter, we can only pluck 4 or 5 kg a day. During the plucking season, we can pick around twenty to 25 kg. There is an old lady in our Line who can pick 80 kg a day.

My husband goes back to his village in Andhra Pradesh every three to five years. His ancestors left that place 150 years ago. He has nothing left there. But he still goes. All of us are like that, the men I mean. We like to still have that link. Many still get married to people from their original village.

This one is my daughter. She started working here only last year. Nowadays, they don't allow anyone below eighteen to work here. But what can we do? The money is not enough. My son has managed to get a job in the police. He is lucky but still it is not enough.

The work is always tough, but especially so in summer. Oh yes, it is hot here when it's summer. It feels like the skin has caught fire. There is

---

[42] A *creole mix of Bengali, Assamese, Hindi, Telugu and Santhal*
[43] A respectful salutation, equivalent to 'Sir'

no wind also. There are many snakes inside these tea trees. Earlier many died from snake bites. Now we have the medicine in our Line. But there is no medicine for mosquito bites. These mosquitoes know our hands are always busy. They know that any time we spend killing them makes us lose money. They know that the Sardar[44] is always watching if we are wasting time. These mosquitoes know how each one of us tastes. They bite us all day. Maybe they have names for us. These are fat, and lazy also. Some don't even bother to fly anymore. They just crawl from one of us to the next one. We are so easy food for them. But when you work in a group and you sing and talk with others, it is bearable.

The women hurried inside the fields once lunch hour was over. With quick wrist movements, they denuded a tea bush of its leaves before one could even finish a breath. They broke into a song and giggled, a common practice while plucking. Jhumur, the songs of the tea-tribes of Assam, are songs of romantic love, the joy of life, or the pain of being a tea worker.

One of the songs goes like this:[45]

'I put my name in the books (contract)
Oh nasty Shyam (Lord Krishna)
You deceived us to Assam
Sardar says work work
Babu says catch that one
Sahib threatens to peel the skin of my back
Oh Jaduram (wizard God)
You deceived us to Assam.'

Rao, twenty-eight, a son of tea-plantation workers, is a migrant worker himself. He worked as a driver in Sri Lanka and was visiting home near Baxung. He took us to the Line in Baxung where he grew up. The Line

---

[44] Word for the manager
[45] PRODUCING TEA COOLIES?: WORK, LIFE AND PROTEST IN THE COLONIAL TEA PLANTATIONS OF ASSAM, 1830S–1920S, Nitin Varma, 1.12.2011

there was made up of rows of houses in pastel blue. The earth was barren and beige, the air dusty, and the whole place seemed like a ghost town.

Rao:

That one was my house. Looks like the same. I haven't come here for six years, ever since I moved out. My mother now lives in the house I bought for her in Jorhat. My father has died.

Living here was tough. They say there is a hospital but where is the doctor? Where are the medicines? Life was hardest during the rains. I remember water dripping from the entire roof, as if the roof is the cloud. Many people died from diseases then. I wish I could have shown you the toilets. They are never cleaned or repaired. They are so bad that no one uses them. My mother had to defecate in the open. A young bride comes here and she has to go and defecate in the open. So when we moved away, everyone was very happy. My father was so proud.

You can see there is no one now in this Line. The whole Line feels like a cemetery. Because everyone is out working. Entire families work in the tea estates. Some are maybe in school now, the younger ones. But they all have to do some work too. I used to make brooms that we sold to shops. They say that the children don't work here anymore and ask the workers to say the same thing. Even those young ones who go to school, they leave school in a few years and start working in the estates, especially the girls. There is no choice. The money is just not enough.

Everyone wants to leave but they can't. The pay is low but we don't have a good education so even if we go outside, we don't get anything better. Many try to work as construction workers. But then they don't get the house or the rations we get here. So we are all locked in. It is very hard to escape. It is too complicated. I was lucky. I left for Mauritius and then to Sri Lanka to work in hotels. But even for me, I had to come back from Mauritius after just a few months because I had to take care of my mother when my father died. I was lucky that I found a job in Sri Lanka later. Others who had managed to escape also have a lot of trouble. Like many young girls from here are stolen by agents and child traffickers. They promise that the girl will work as an airhostess or in a hotel, that the money will be good, but then these girls end up as prostitutes or are forced to marry some old man in faraway Delhi, Punjab or Mumbai. Sometimes, the family knows but they also lie to the girl, they just want to have one less mouth to feed. Sometimes, the girl knows but still goes because she thinks it is more glamorous outside. Some girls just run away. Some boys also.

During the ULFA[46] days, they were killing us Bagania people. They called us outsiders then. We were so scared. Any moment, their people could suddenly come into a Line and shoot all the men. But nowadays, everyone loves baganiya people. Politicians from all parties come and say baganiya people are their brothers and sisters. They play our songs and dances and call it local Assamese culture. Now we are not outsiders anymore. Because now, there is a new common enemy, the Bangladeshi. Some Bangladeshis came and tried to find work in the plantations. But last year, they were all driven out. Don't ask me by whom.

Yes, now everybody loves us Baganias. But has anything really changed for my people? Nothing ever changes.

---

[46] The United Liberation Front of Assam (ULFA) ran a violent insurgency campaign for independence of the state from India. They were most active during the early 1990s

Now I Live with an 'Alien' Face

*Ataur Rahman (Bangladesh), twenty-seven year old,
Self-employed, former Landscape Worker in Singapore*

I was born in a small village in Pabna district in Bangladesh. I have two brothers and one sister. I am the eldest. My father was an agricultural labourer. We didn't have our own land. We were always very poor. I didn't want to end up working as an agricultural labourer as well. I wanted to change my life. Many young people from our village had left for Singapore as migrant workers. I thought of doing the same.

I took a loan and joined a training centre. I passed my exam in one attempt and landed in Singapore in 2015.

In Singapore, I was working for a landscaping company. The company's boss liked me. But my supervisor—a Bangladeshi like me—used to give me the toughest tasks. On 25 July 2016, I had an accident.

I don't think my company ever followed many safety guidelines. The boss and the supervisor had built a rainwater storage tank all by themselves. I am not sure if it was built properly. That evening, my supervisor asked me and a few others to thoroughly clean the whole tank. He said that no matter how much time it took, we must remove all the water from inside and make sure that the tank was spanking clean. I didn't know anything about water storage tanks. And I didn't know much about safety as well; I had just attended one day of safety training. I didn't understand much. Yet, when I entered the tank, I felt as if I couldn't breathe. It was a big tank, almost like two rooms joined together. It was very dark inside. The air was strange. I asked if we could clean during the day instead. The supervisor said, 'Do you want to stay in Singapore? If yes, then go inside and clean, else get a ticket out of Singapore for tomorrow.' My salary was only 700–800 Singapore dollars and I had a big loan. What could I say?

I took an electric light with a long cable and went inside the tank. The moment I turned on the switch for the light, there was a big explosion. I was thrown away. I don't know what happened. Maybe there was some gas inside the tank. The explosion was so powerful. I just knew that some people were dragging me out. I had more than seventy per cent burns. My flesh had boiled. When the people pulled me out, my skin stuck to their hands. The last thing I remember was being taken out of an ambulance. Then I went into a coma for three months.

When I came back to my senses, I couldn't see anything. It was all dark. I felt like I was locked in a dark room. I couldn't talk. I couldn't move. They had tied my hands and legs. They said that I was moving too much and I could hurt myself. I couldn't eat anything. I couldn't drink. The only sense I had was that of hearing. I remember hearing the sound of flowing water, perhaps nurses washing hands after they did something with my bandages. I could feel the presence of people. They were moving around me. They were talking among themselves. I couldn't ask them anything.

Those days, lying all day in the bed, what could I do but think? And what does one think when left all alone? I thought I would never be able to speak again. I would never be able to walk again. What was the point of living then? I couldn't even manage my own bodily functions. Why didn't I just die from the accident? I can't explain how much I suffered.

After many days, they opened my eyes. I could see just a little. I couldn't talk yet. There was a tube cut into my throat to help with breathing and feeding. I felt so thirsty all the time. They fed me water only through the tube. I wanted so much to take a big gulp and feel how it feels to swallow water. Well, if only I could take just a sip of water, just a sip. But the nurse wouldn't allow it. It was like this for one month. It felt so horrible.

My doctor was a very good person. She encouraged me a lot. She asked me to stay positive. She assured me again and again that the treatment was working. She explained in detail the procedures she could do on me and how I would recover bit by bit. They asked for my permission before undertaking anything. I couldn't write yet. And I had lost my fingerprints in the accident. So they used to take the print from my toes.

I spent another three months in the hospital. I just remember being taken away to the operation table every now and then. I can't add up how many times I was operated upon. There was surgery for the eyelid, for lips, for hair. Every inch of my body got cut and sewed. Slowly, I began to recover. I could walk. I could move around. I thought that I had a chance. I felt that I might live.

One day, I finally saw my full face in a mirror. But who was this person in front of me? I didn't know him at all. My eyes had shrunk from all the surgery. My lips were deformed. I was looking so strange. I had become an alien!

Killing time in the hospital was so difficult. For how long can one stay asleep? I would wake up at eight in the morning, and then wait for the nurses to feed me like a baby. Then I had to find a way to spend time till the next meal. I had a cheap Chinese phone. It had stopped working because of not being charged for three months while I was in coma. My room had a TV but the hospital had only a few free TV channels. The programs were in English, Chinese, Malay or Tamil. I couldn't understand any of these. I couldn't press the remote either so the nurses put on whatever I requested. Because of some cultural similarities, I asked for the Tamil programs. These were only shown in the afternoon. I didn't understand anything but that was all I could do.

For much of this time, I couldn't contact my family. They had heard from other migrant workers that I had had an accident. They were convinced that I had died. For migrant workers who die while working overseas, their dead bodies were typically sent back to Bangladesh only after a few months. So if people told my family that I was still alive, they just didn't believe it. My parents would accuse them that they were just giving false hopes. My parents became like mad. Only after they spoke to me, they believed that I wasn't dead.

The supervisor from my company visited me once in a while. He tried to be nice. But I didn't like talking to him. In my heart, I knew that my condition was because of their carelessness. In any case, I couldn't speak yet.

In total, I was in the hospital for six months. But even after my release, I had to get treated regularly and even get operated for face reconstruction a few times. The company refused to pay more than what their insurance covered, a mere 36,000 Singapore dollars. My hospital bill was running into many hundreds of thousands of dollars. The company refused to pay. The hospital chased me for payment. The hospital's social worker linked me with an NGO called HOME. They helped me a lot. I am really grateful to them. I still have many friends there. I talk to them on zoom even now. I even came to one of their volunteer's wedding.

After I was released from the hospital, HOME asked me to join them as a volunteer interpreter. I agreed. I used to sit at their office every day. At HOME, I got to know so many unfortunate cases of other migrant workers. I didn't, however, come across anyone who had as bad an accident as mine. But it is not so simple. Many workers have seemingly minor accidents; you can't see any injury marks on their body but the person just drops dead. In my case, I had very visible injuries; but I survived. I got support from NGOs. I got some compensation. But many workers don't even get any compensation. They don't get any treatment. They come back to Bangladesh but have no money to see a doctor here. Like there was a boy who had a broken back. He couldn't even walk. The company denied that it was a worksite accident. So the boy didn't get any treatment. I think employers always have the upper hand. So in a way, many workers suffer worse than me.

I worked with HOME till 2018 and then I came back to Bangladesh. Once back, I couldn't comprehend what to do. How could I make a living? I was clueless. I paid off my loans with the compensation money that I got from the company. I used some of it to buy some cows and start a farm. My family is still doing farm work. With whatever was left from my compensation money, I started a school. This has always been my dream. In Bangladesh, we have so many problems with education. Especially for those poor children in rural areas; they are very bad at reading. Forget English, they can't even read Bengali. So I always wanted to do something to improve this situation. I teach the kids English and computers by myself. There are other teachers for other subjects. Today, the school has about 200 students. I hope my school can grow.

I don't like to think about the past much. What has happened has happened. I got married last year. Now I am a new person. My face is different from before. This face always surprises me when I look at the mirror. But other than that, I can do all my work. I can take care of myself. I can work hard. So I don't like to think about the past anymore. My only advice to migrant workers is to always prioritize safety and be cautious when working. Many come under pressure to follow every command of their employer; they feel the burden of loans for high agent fees and fear that they would be sent back if they decline to do so. They take risks even when they know it is wrong, it is dangerous. I wish I could tell them my story.

I Paid for all Their Education. And Now They Say I'm Worthless

Mehedi Hassan (Bangladesh), thirty-three years old, unemployed, former Construction Worker in Singapore

I come from a village named Nahali. Nahali is located in Tangail district in Bangladesh. My father used to work in the army. I have one brother and one sister. I am the eldest. I studied till Senior Secondary School and then came to Singapore in 2009.

My father was cheated by all his siblings. He was the eldest and helped to raise all his ten brothers and sisters. Despite this, they swindled him of all his money. They even fought with him and disowned him. He suffered a lot because of them. He couldn't realize his dream of working abroad because of them. He lost all his savings because of them. I wanted to avenge him and realize his dream. But as a child, I too wanted to join the army like my father. But then I fell in love with a girl. She didn't love me. Or I think she did love me but didn't express it. If I had joined the army, it would have been impossible to marry her because it would have taken too long to make enough money to ask for her hand. So I thought that if I worked in Singapore for four or five years then I would be able to save enough. Because of these two reasons, I came to Singapore. But only once I was in Singapore, I realized what it means to be in a foreign country.

I first joined a marine company in Singapore and then I worked in a construction company. One day, in 2011, I was sitting in front of the lorry and then there was an accident; shards of glass went into my head. The company got me treated but later I got to know that the company had swallowed the entire insurance claim while not giving me anything. Then a few months later, I had another accident. I slipped on the wet floor while working and then my upper lip burst. I needed seven stitches. Then all of a sudden, the company asked me to leave, without giving any reason.

I joined another construction company and worked there for two years. I hardly made any money there because the pay was so low. People become migrant workers only to make money; but I just wasted time.

I was working in scaffolding. Such work is extremely hard. I couldn't even drink water while working. Because of this, I got jaundice. I became very weak. I fell sick. I came back to Bangladesh. I spent a lot of money to get myself treated. For one and a half years I did whatever any doctor asked me to do. But whenever I tried to get a permit to work again in Singapore, they would say that I was medically unfit.

Finally, after I recovered, I came back to Singapore to work for a manpower supplier company. Within three months, I had another accident. I was given the task of digging a drain. It was very hot and I was tired. And they were rushing me to work fast. My spade hit some rock. I fell down into the drain and then rolled down some distance. I think my wrist got dislocated and I was also hurt in my head and neck. The company took me to some company doctor. They didn't file any safety reports. They asked me to not mention anything about head and neck, only about the hand. They said they would take me to some other doctor for my head and neck. But later they said that I was fine. They didn't get me treated anymore. But I was feeling a lot of pain and so one night I went with my friend to another hospital. They did an MRI and then operated upon me. I took money from friends to pay for all this.

When I showed my company the report from the new doctor, they got furious. They drove me around all day and then finally went to the new hospital that I was seeing. There they challenged this new doctor and asked him to cancel my MC (Medical Leave Certificate). They kept saying that they will send me to Bangladesh. Then I gave a call to the police. One of the officers who came asked me to complain to MOM.[47] I followed his suggestion.

I got ten points for my injury, five for head and five for neck. But for my hand, which was a big operation, I got zero points. Also my pay was low and so I only got 12,400 Singapore dollars of which I had to pay 1,800 to my lawyer. All this was happening during the early days of COVID-19 when I was locked up in the dormitory like most other workers. The company didn't even want to give me proper food because of my complaint. I got fed up, accepted the ten points, and just came back to Bangladesh.

Since then, I have not been doing anything. I am struggling to get a job. I just roam around, eat, and sleep. I still have difficulty with my hand. My money is running out fast. Now I am a useless person. My parents think I am worthless. My brother and sister think I am worthless.

I got married three months back. People say that sons behave differently with their parents once they get married. I am telling you that it is the other way. Within fifteen days of getting married, my parents and my siblings started behaving differently with me. When I first came to Singapore, my siblings were very young. I paid for all their education. One has already graduated with honours and the other is pursuing the same. But now that I have no money, despite having done so much for them, they say so many things like, 'You couldn't help us with this, you could have helped us with that. You went overseas but what have you achieved?' Oh, they say so many nasty things . . .

I am not well . . . I am not at peace . . .

What advice can I give others who want to migrate? Only once someone has migrated, can he understand the reality. When I first came to Singapore, I was such a novice. I had so many hopes. I have seen and experienced a lot as a migrant. A migrant life cannot be called a life. Every migrant has so many hopes but not many can fulfil them.

---

[47] Ministry of Manpower, Singapore

You may say that people like me should stay in my country and work there. But if you give me that advice or even if the Prime Minister of Bangladesh gives me that advice, then I will ask just one question, will you feed me, will you take care of my family? There are so many unemployed people in Bangladesh, even among those who are highly educated. Even if someone wants to do something in Bangladesh it costs a lot of money. Just to start a shop takes 50,000 or 60,000 Singapore dollars. I don't even have ten thousand, how can I dream of 50,000. I want to get my wife educated but even that costs so much. And you may say that I should take up some manual jobs in Bangladesh, just like I used to do in Singapore. But I am from a middle-class family. I can't work in the fields, or in day jobs, or as a driver here. People will say so many things. They will say you are from this family and look at what you are doing. So what can I do? So I have no advice for anyone who wants to leave Bangladesh. I can't tell them to not go because I understand their situation. Just go and find out for yourself.

That's why I need to go back to Singapore but my application to return keeps getting rejected. Or perhaps, I could go somewhere in Europe. I heard Singaporeans know many people in Europe and Europeans give a lot of value to their words. Can you talk to some Europeans about me?

I'm Hurt, But Please Don't Send Me Back

Mamun (Bangladesh), twenty-eight year old, former Construction Worker in Singapore

I was born in Kushtia district in Bangladesh. I have a younger sister. My father is a farmer and my mother is a homemaker. We didn't have our own land. My father was a day labourer. We were poor.

I was a good student. I had joined college to pursue a degree in economics. But I couldn't continue because of financial reasons. It was impossible for my father to support my higher education. A day labourer like him struggles even to put enough food onto the plates of family members.

Many men from my village were working overseas. Taking their cue, I thought of joining a training centre so I could come to Singapore. The training centre asked for 70,000 taka. I borrowed money and joined one. The people at the training centre used to beat us a lot. Every time we made a mistake, they would hit us with wooden planks. They wanted us to pass the exam for Singapore as soon as possible.

This was back in 2013. Around then, the political situation in Bangladesh became tense. Every day there were riots, strikes, and violence. We heard rumours that employers from Singapore won't come to Bangladesh till the situation improves. After six months at the training centre, I finally got to take the exam. I cleared it at the first attempt. But in order to get the IPA[48] to come to Singapore, I needed my passport. When we had joined the training centre, it had kept our passports. Now they asked me to pay 400,000 taka to give it back. Where could I get so much money? I borrowed again.

Eventually, I got my IPA but they demanded another 225,000 taka before they would release it to me. So I borrowed again. Finally, on 17 September 2013, I landed in Singapore.

I had thought that the employer would give me some clerical job or perhaps I would serve tea or snacks to their staff. But they put me on a construction job. I got to know this only when they took me to the site on my first day at work. That very day, they asked me to dig out pipes from the muddy ground. It was so hard. The mud stuck in big lumps to the spade. I struggled to manage. I had never done anything like this before. I had no clue. I cried that day.

I would cry often because of the work I was doing. They made me lift heavy rods. I had to work in rain, in mud, under hot sun, all that. I was studying economics and this is how I had ended up. But there was no way out. I had borrowed so much. I had to continue.

Within a year, I managed to repay 500,000 taka of my loans. But then I heard that the company will send us back. Apparently they didn't have enough work. I cried again. There was a foreman from Bangladesh and I cried in front of him. I begged him to keep me at work and renew my permit. I asked him to take pity on me. Nothing worked. In September 2014, I was sent back to Bangladesh. I started working as a day labourer, just like my father.

Nine months later, I managed to get a new IPA for Singapore. This time, I had to pay another 8,000 Singapore dollars. So I had to borrow again. 11 June 2015, I was back.

In my new job, I had to carry heavy bags full of cement. This time I was determined to continue. No matter how hard the work, I had to

---

[48] In-Principle Approval

stay in Singapore. I had to take care of my family. Again I managed to repay another 500,000 taka of my loans within just one year.

But the same thing happened again. Once more, I begged the foreman, this time a Chinese, to keep me in the company. I even offered him some money. Nothing worked. For the second time, I became a failure in Singapore.

My father got irritated and said that there was no point looking for work in Singapore, 'Let's just work in the fields, we will work together, raise some goats, and then we can pay back the loans.' This time, my parents were very determined. But I told my mother that let this be the last time. Let me try just once more. She helped to convince my father.

This time, I got the IPA within two months. It also cost less, around 4,000 Singapore dollars. After six months, the employer asked me if I had any certificates. I said yes, for lifting supervisor. They took my interview and changed my job to that of a lifting supervisor. My salary became quite decent. Soon I had only 200,000 taka of unpaid loans. I was doing well.

10 March 2017, 10 a.m.; I had an accident. I was supervising lifting and shifting. The crane operator made a mistake. He moved the crane-arm too fast. The blade swung and hit me hard. I was hurt badly. I felt such pain. But what was the first thing on my mind? Will they send me back to Bangladesh?

The safety officer came. I begged him, 'Don't send me back to Bangladesh. I want to work.' He said, 'Okay, don't worry, you get well.' They took me to a hospital. They kept me under observation for a few hours and then moved me to a big hospital. The nurse told me, 'You have had a big accident; they will operate on you tonight.' The doctor gave me an injection and asked me many questions. He asked me my level of pain on a scale of one to ten. I said eight. Then they moved me to the ICU. But they didn't operate.

After ten days, they moved me to the general ward. I was feeling a little better. The doctor said that this hospital was expensive and my boss didn't want to pay so much, so they wanted to move me back to the earlier hospital, the smaller one. I agreed.

Two days later, I started having unbelievable pain in my stomach. I can't tell you in words how much pain. I couldn't tolerate it. At twelve in the night they sent me back to the bigger hospital. There, the doctor gave some medicine and I felt a bit better. The next day they sent me again to the cheaper hospital. They were only worried about cost. Whenever I felt bad, they sent me to the bigger hospital. The moment I felt slightly better, they took me back to the cheaper one.

On 30 March, they sent me back to the dormitory. I couldn't eat properly yet. If I ate something, I would vomit. And I couldn't pass urine or excrete without pain. That night at the dormitory, I had rice for dinner. Shortly thereafter, I had terrible pain in my stomach. I can't describe it. I was screaming. The next morning, I told my safety supervisor what had happened. Again, I was sent to the cheaper hospital. I told the supervisor, 'Whatever you do, please don't send me to Bangladesh. If you send me back, I will just have to commit suicide'.

After staying for five or six days in the hospital, the nature of my pain changed. I would be okay but then suddenly I would feel like my stomach would burst. The supervisor came to meet me. He said, 'Brother, you are more or less okay, why don't you go back to Bangladesh? If you stay with your parents, they will take care of you, you will recover faster, then you can come back to Singapore within fifteen days. We will pay you 100,000 taka.'

I knew it was a trick, to send me back for good. I said, 'No no, don't send me back, the incident happened in Singapore, so I should recover in Singapore.' My friends and relatives in Singapore also came to support me. They repeated to the supervisor what I was saying. Eventually he backed down.

On 12 April, I went for a check-up. The doctor asked how I was feeling. I told him that I still had a lot of pain. He thought for a while and then suddenly said that I have to get operated immediately, as soon as possible, else I might not live. He called my boss and said something in Chinese. On 13 April, they operated on me.

A few days after the surgery, a lot of pus developed around my stitches from the operation. When the doctor saw this, he said,

'Oh my god'. They changed my dressing every day. But skin and muscles began to fall off from my wound. On May 8, they sent me back to the cheaper hospital. I couldn't say anything. What could I do?

I spent four months and seventeen days between various hospitals. As I couldn't eat, they used to feed me through the nose. That was very painful. I couldn't move on my own for two months. I peed on the bed. I was just lying down all day. I got bed sores. I would fall asleep and then wake up thinking I had slept for fifteen hours. But when I saw the clock, it was only two hours. Time just wouldn't pass. You can't imagine, I used to look at the clock over 1,000 times every day. Sometimes I would dream of Bangladesh. I would imagine having my own farm there. I didn't want to die in Singapore. I wanted to see my parents for one last time before dying.

When I was in the ICU, I used to tell my parents that I was just having a fever and so I was lying down. I didn't tell them anything about the accident. But at some point they got to know everything because there were many workers from my village in Singapore. My parents became crazy. Every day, they wept till midnight. Sometimes they just roamed aimlessly around our village, like mad people.

Eventually, I recovered a bit but not fully. So they sent me back to the dormitory. I was certain that the company would terminate my job and send me back, even though I was recovering a bit. I felt that I may not be able to do such manual work anymore. So if I got some compensation from the company, at least I could repay some of the loans and maybe run some small business in Bangladesh. I consulted with an NGO called TWC2 and also filed a case against the company. Following the NGO's advice, I went back to Bangladesh while the case was still ongoing. Eventually I settled for an offer of 85,000 Singapore dollars from the company.

I used the settlement money to buy and rear some cows in my village. I have also started two small businesses related to jute and tobacco. I don't have any experience in business. I have incurred big losses already in the tobacco business. I got married last year. We are expecting a child in seven months. My money is running away fast. I have been a failure so far. Everything I touch, I make a loss.

I miss Singapore so much. And I miss all the people in the NGO who helped me. When I see images of Singapore on TV, I get such strong feelings, like I was in this street, and I have been there, or I used to eat there. But sometimes I wonder, will I ever be able to come back?

I have only one piece of advice for other migrant workers—Safety first!

Could I Have Saved My Best Friend's Life?

Durga Balan (India), thirty-five years old, Safety Officer in Singapore

I was born in Tamil Nadu, India, in a village called Moovalur near the big city of Thanjavur. My father was an engineer, my mother a homemaker. I have a younger brother who works as a software engineer in India. My wife is also a homemaker. She has a Masters in Commerce. We have a son and a daughter. My family still lives in Moovalur.

In 2008, I came to Singapore as a technician in a manufacturing company. I am now a safety officer in the petrochemical sector. I hardly go out. After I finish my work, I just come to my room. Some days, if it is a holiday, I go to a temple outside. Sometimes I go out to take photographs, sometimes I play badminton. Most of my free time, I stay inside my room. There I read books related to my courses. That's about it. I am reaching forty. At this age, we shouldn't waste time. I sent back all my savings. I only leave some for my food and rent and for my courses.

The agent money is the key factor in deciding whether to come to Singapore as a migrant worker and how long you should stay. You need to calculate how many years you need to work to get back the agent money. You need to consider the interest also if you borrow to pay the agent money. So after all this, you have to calculate how much you are going to get as salary, how much you are going to spend here, and so how much balance you would have to send back to your hometown. Say for example, if you pay 6,000 Singapore dollars as agent money, then there is the interest, then at the end of month, if you get only 650 dollars as salary, then expenses add up to a minimum of 200 dollars, on room, on phone, on food, so almost only after one and a half years, you can start sending money home. Of course, if you have a higher salary, you can come. I could pay back my agent money in seven months. Secondly, based on my personal experience, if you step into Singapore, you need to think about your career development. You can come as a general worker but then slowly learn the things that are happening around you. Study something, upgrade to a higher level, so that from a general worker, you can become a supervisor. I saw many of my friends come as general workers and become Project Managers. But I also know many who just don't want to upgrade. Their friends have become supervisors while they are still only general workers. So don't get stuck in the same position. This is not my advice, just suggestions for those who want to come to Singapore as migrant workers. Don't just put yourself in the same place; you need to move up.

But you can plan all this and then things can also go horribly wrong. As a safety officer, I have seen many bad things. My family doesn't know about the dangers at my work. My habit is to not tell them anything about my work, especially to my wife or mother. Otherwise, they will worry. They will take it more seriously than what it is.

But I cannot forget two accidents in particular. One day, I was working at a site and in the very opposite facility; I saw a sudden burst of fire at my eye level, conical in shape. It lasted barely a second or less. Two workers, both from India, were badly injured. We rushed to recover them. We needed to open their shirts, but it was stuck to their body. So I used scissors to cut one man's shirt. His skin came out with the shirt. Really, really, the skin came out from his hands, his back, his chest, from everywhere. It was so terrible to see this. Their safety boots had melted into their legs. It was so terrible. They survived. But they were in the hospital for many months.

But more significantly, on 15 October, last year, my best friend got caught in an accident. For five years, we had worked on the same projects. He was a supervisor while I was the safety officer. When we were working together, I would always remind him of safety practices. But sometimes, he would become too engrossed at work and skip a safety measure or two. At the time of the accident, we were not working together. There was another safety officer with him. At 11.30 in the morning, I got a call from this other safety officer. He told me that there was an accident in my facility and the lifting supervisor had died. Then I realized, what, the dead man was my best friend. A very high and heavy beam had fallen on him. He had died on the spot. For three months, I was in a total mess. I just couldn't forget him. I couldn't sleep well. I couldn't eat properly. I couldn't work. Even after my father had passed away, I didn't feel so bad. But I cried only for him. People asked why I was behaving like this; he was just a friend. But I can't think like that. When his mother died, he couldn't go back to India. He had also not seen his son who was only three months old at the time of his death. I had asked him to take leave and go see his baby but he didn't. After that incident, whenever I saw someone wearing that uniform and working in the lifting zone, I kept thinking about him. Would it have been different if I was with him that day? Really, really, I just couldn't work there anymore. So I joined a different company. Since then, I have recovered a bit. But I still can't forget him. He was such a kind hearted person. He thought of everyone just as human beings. His name is Muniyan Murugan. Please mention his name in your book.

Part V

Migrant workers are often placed in situations where their colleagues and employers come from a mesh of unfamiliar cultures, religions, languages, and food habits. What prejudices do they have to face in such a context? Are migrant workers able to shed their own biases? How do cultural misunderstandings lead to unfavourable work outcomes? Can true friendship and a sense of camaraderie still emerge from this milieu?

In this section, the featured migrant workers—Zhou BoTong, Zhou Hongxing, Blissful Life (China), Md Sharif (Bangladesh); Anirban and Arun (India)—dwell on these questions and more as they narrate their life stories.

Call My Story a 'Diary of Blood and Sweat in Nanyang'

Zhou BoTong (name changed), China, forty-one years old, Construction Worker in Singapore

My life? My life is a mess. I'm so happy to find someone to tell it all—a stranger. If I talk to a familiar person, he'll laugh at me.

Call my story 'Diary of blood and sweat in Nanyang'[49]. Let my story be known to the world, become as famous as *Journey to the West*. Call me by my pen name, Zhou Botong[50]. I don't know where to start . . . I am too complex. I was born in Shanxi, in the plains. After I stopped my studies, I went fucking around. I did all kinds of jobs—labourer, bricklayer. When I made a bit of money, I opened my own restaurant despite not having any experience. Then I bought my own truck to transport medicine and grains. I couldn't make any money in these and then had an accident because of drink-driving.

After the accident I was down for more than half a year. My old woman[51] said, 'Go make some money overseas'. Hey, she was right!

---

[49] South ocean, referred to Singapore
[50] The name of a character from Jin Yong's story, literally means 'Old mischievous boy'
[51] Wife

I finally did make some money once I went overseas. I have been a migrant worker ever since.

In 2015, I came to Singapore for the first time. I had to pay 20,000 yuan to an employment agency in Shandong. They put me through training. I cared a fuck about the studies or exams, just had fun every day. I never passed any of the mock exams. I totally couldn't make it. Teacher Li said, 'You should just go home to repair the planet[52], this job is not for you.' I was thinking, what the fuck is 'not for me'?

The teacher was really nasty. He beat me on my head, kicked me . . . scolded me saying I didn't know this and that. I said, 'If I knew everything then why would I come to study here? What is the meaning of the word "study" then? And are you behaving like a teacher? Fucking hell, you can talk all you like, but why beat me with tools? For just one hell of a job? Honestly, why should you care about me passing or not, if I didn't even care? You are not going to refund me a cent of that 20,000 yuan either way.'

I didn't study at all before the exam. I drank wine for two full days and took the wine bottles along to the exam. The teacher got super scared that I might hit him with the bottles. I said, 'Don't say anything. Anything you say will just be a fart. I'm not happy. I have paid the money to come and learn. You didn't teach me properly . . . Don't worry, I am an adult, I can drink a lot. I won't violate the law. If you beat me, you are violating the law . . . '

After the exam, I drank to my heart's content and went to sleep. The next day they told me that I had passed. They said I should celebrate. I asked, 'What's the big deal?' He apologized to me. I said, 'Thank you. Somehow, you taught me. You had your difficulties.'

My first job in Singapore was that of a carpenter. A carpenter is the same as a labourer. I had to carry heavy boards. You cannot do the work without knowing physics well. Otherwise, you will fall and get hurt. Because of the hot and humid weather, I had severe eczema all over my body. I took pictures of my private parts. Do you see all the wounds? I worked for ten months with my teeth clenched . . . and

---

[52] An insult saying someone is useless

finally I couldn't take it and went back to China. I lost around 20 kg, no longer looked like my ID card. When I went back to China, the immigration officer looked at me and said, 'Is this the same person?' I was totally deformed.

I tried going to South Korea. A friend was already working there. The agent arranged for me to travel as a fake visitor to the Winter Olympics. It was agreed that I would pay one tranche of the agent fees only after landing. But the agent suddenly asked me to pay before boarding the flight, saying they'd give me back that money in Korean Won after landing. I told them I was not going to Korea any more. They refused to return my documents nor refund my earlier payments. I said, whatever. I don't want the money any more. You keep it.

Then I thought of going to Sri Lanka. On Baidu[53], it said that Sri Lanka was an oriental teardrop, as beautiful as the Maldives. In an agent's advertisement they said that one could go to Sri Lanka within two-three months after paying their fees. This time, I paid a bloody sum of 3,000 yuan. Nothing happened for one whole year. I went with others to fight with the agent. They let their dogs out to attack us. After a lot of fighting, they gave me back the money. Still, I wish I had gone to Sri Lanka for a few days. It sounded like such a good place. But those who went said that I was lucky to not have gone there. There was no work there anyway. Sigh, life is full of traps.

Thereafter, a friend introduced me to a job at a scallop farm at Ocean Island in Dalian. He said that so-and-so made over 100,000 yuan in just one year. I thought that was great. No need to go overseas, I can bring my wife as well.

At Ocean Island, we raised scallops that began their life the size as small as a rice grain. As they grew, we transferred them from a small walled cage to a bigger one, and then to an even bigger one. It was pure labour. The walled cages were enormous. The empty cages put for drying stacked up like big mountains.

We'd go out in boats to place these cages in the Huanghai sea. Most of the time we floated on the sea. We had to get up at 4.30 a.m. and

---

[53] Search Engine in China

work well beyond midnight. Every day. This was the most important period in the entire year for farm owners, these months of July and August. They needed things done so they could make their money. It was hard work. It was hot like hell on the shore. It was also hot like hell in the boats. When the big waves came up, the boats shook violently. I didn't know how to swim. All I had was a yellow vest on me. What use could that be? Nobody would save me if I really fell into the sea.

I had terrible seasickness. At first, I took five pills a day, then eight . . . ten pills . . . no use. My head and eyes became blurred . . . I would throw up my entire stomach every day.

I said, I want to go home. The leader was a fucking smiling tiger[54], fucking idiot. He told me that they'd pay 100,000 yuan if I stayed till the end of the year. I'd get just 50 yuan a day if I stopped before that. Fuck his grandma . . . I worked like hell for eight months, just for 3,000 yuan? I could have made that in a month anywhere else!

Initially, there were around 500 people working at the farm. They left one by one. I was among the last men standing. I wanted to persevere till the end and take some money home. But I was risking my life. I vomited for three days and three nights. I was unable to eat anything. Some people fainted and then went back to work after waking up. I'd say, working like that . . . what for . . . not that it's huge money . . .

It wasn't easy to leave Ocean Island. There were ferries back to the city only on Monday, Wednesday, and Friday mornings. Even on those days, the ferries would not come if there was fog on the sea. I was stuck for two weeks. I had splitting headaches. Heaven or hell never answered me. This was the saddest situation I've ever been in.

After that, I worked as a temporary worker in a bus factory. A year later, they asked if I wanted to become permanent. But they said 'My salary had to walk down a bit'. I got angry and left. Damn it! I'll go to Singapore again.

I came back to Singapore for the second time, once again as a carpenter. And again came the eczema. It lasted for more than a

---

[54] Chinese proverb, referred to nasty people who appear friendly

year . . . My private parts were full of rashes . . . again, like children's diaper rashes. When my skin rubbed against clothes . . . that pain, I cannot describe. All the time, I walk with my legs open. 99.9 per cent of migrant workers from China have this, especially us people from Northern China who are used to having colder seasons. We work under the big sun; it is too hot. There is no escape. It is us who have to try to adapt to Singapore, we cannot ask Singapore to adapt to us.

Every morning, we wake up really early, then wait for the bus at 5 a.m., sleep a bit in the bus, then start working at 8 a.m. There are many routine checks; sign on timesheet, safety certificate, take temperature, Trace Together[55], tap time-card . . . . We have lunch at 12 p.m., and then work from 1 p.m. to 9 p.m. We take dinner back to our dormitory and eat there. Between lunch and dinner, there's no food. I get hungry around 4–5 p.m. I buy soft drinks or eat a few biscuits and that's it. It's natural you'll be hungry around then, even if not working. Even more so because I don't feel like eating my lunch—noon is too hot to eat.

My life is tough, other people's lives are tougher. All Chinese workers are in this fucking situation. It's hard to earn money, but even harder to eat shit. The words are ugly but the idea is not. What to do, who asked you to be poor?

The thing I love most about Singapore is that every month, we receive our salary. In China, I used to work hard for one whole year without getting paid. Here, I get the money on time, and nothing else matters. Sigh, but here, our rice is not even cooked. The company buys cheap food for us from Pasar[56]. I eat half-cooked rice all year long. I even need to buy my own working boots. $38 per pair. One pair lasts only two months. To save money, I buy things in the biggest packaging; two huge bottles of shampoo, one huge 25 kg pack of laundry powder that looks like a bag of fertilizer. Then there's the phone data cost. I hardly buy any clothes except for underwear. I consume a lot of socks. It's impossible to wear working boots without socks. I buy myself a treat in the restaurants only once every one or two months.

---

[55] COVID-19 tracker in Singapore
[56] Local market

'Ay, come! Number 248, Number 1227!' Our company calls us by numbers. Everyone is a number. Tell me how can we get any respect? So funny. Damn it. It's just me who still thinks of myself as a human.

I'm embarrassed that I still don't know who's who in my dormitory room, after one whole year. I know only the name of the guy on the bed next to mine, not of the two others sharing the same bunk bed with me. Every day, we finish work, wash up, watch the phone, and sleep. We don't talk! Nobody cares about others. If you don't wake up on time for work, no one even cares to wake you up. Such is life in a dormitory. People used to be better. When I came to Singapore for the first time, I celebrated Chinese New Year with two fellow workers from the same area in China. We bought two cartons of beer, three mantou, and one side dish. Now we have all parted ways and I no longer know their whereabouts.

In my worksite, there is a Bangla[57]. He is my good workmate. My English is kind of okay. He knows some Chinese words, like good and bad. But we have telepathy. Just make a gesture and we'll understand each other.

Whenever I win in the casino, I buy drinks for the 'blackies'[58]. They ask me why. I just smile, saying, 'I won't tell you, I'm happy. I'm generous.'

Once I won 2,000 Singapore dollars. I sent it home. I was very happy that I sent money to my wife twice in the same month. I told her that it was from working overtime. Didn't dare to mention casinos. After that my charm didn't work anymore. I lost 200 or 300 dollars here and there. Some days back, I won 800, then I lost it all. Even today I lost 180. Let me share some with you if I win again.

I must tell you about my uncle. He has worked in Singapore for twenty-five years. He owns houses and cars in his hometown. He has property in the big city of Bao Ding as well. My wife says I should learn from him. That man didn't go home either for his own mother's funeral or his eldest son's wedding. He only went home after the birth

---

[57] Workers from Bangladesh
[58] A derogatory reference to South Asians

of his grandson. That time, the two daughters-in-law demanded he buy cars for them. They pulled their father-in-law to the 4S shop[59] . The salesgirl asked for a deposit. My uncle said, 'Can you see if there's enough money in my card? If yes, I'll pay in full.' He paid in full. 'What's your job?' the salesgirl asked. 'I'm just a migrant worker,' he said. 'What work do you do to make so much money?' she asked. 'Do you know how much money you have in the card?' He said, 'I don't. Don't ask me anymore, just give it back to me. I have to fly back to Singapore to work.'

I met him once. That time, my wife had asked him to bring some medicine for me. I invited him to have a meal together. He said, 'Don't waste money.' I said, 'Uncle, you have bought apartments for both sons, now you need to buy for your grandson also.' He said, 'Yeah, I have to save for the down payment for my grandson.' I said, 'Why not full payment? You should live a few more years and make sure that even your great-grandsons are also taken care of. Ha-ha.'

There's zero fun in his life. He's the only person I admire in this world. He can do bricklaying, bar-placing, and welding. He works on sewage. He mixes metals. He's just working, working. He leads a few 'blackies'. He has also become dark-skinned like a Bangla. He makes 4,000 plus Singapore dollars a month. He doesn't rest a day. Only such people can make money. True. He's a tycoon. Both his sons don't want to work, they are just eating off their dad.

So, my wife says that it will be great if I can be even half the person he is. I said, 'Forget it. I don't want to. Go easy on me.'

I don't have much interaction with the locals. The only locals I interact with sometimes are those from the church.

I'm not a believer, or you may say I am. I joined a church in Singapore, even got baptized. I used to go there frequently before COVID-19. During the big quarantine in our dormitory, the church people came to give us medicines for free. They even asked me to take some for my workmates. I said, 'I have never

---

[59] Car dealership

even talked to them before, just give me my share.' They said, 'No, please pass these on.'

I don't know why but I always have this bible in my pocket. Sometimes I browse a few pages. I haven't finished reading the whole book till today. This paragraph in the Lord's Prayer touches my heart: ' . . . You will be done on earth as it is in heaven, give us today our daily bread . . . and lead us not into temptation, but deliver us from the evil one . . . now and forever, amen!' I can't fully understand it. Just feel it's nice every time I have to say it. Now I don't go to church. I have started to forget the prayer. I believe that God is everywhere and is always looking after me. I was in dangerous situations a few times but I was saved every time. Like when I had too little sleep and almost fell down from a building . . . God must be helping me. He hasn't abandoned me. Even though I am such a big sinner.

The church people are good people. Sometimes we just talk, or just do prayers. I also learned some Singapore-style English from them. Singaporeans are actually nice and patient. It's just that they don't give you face. Very rigid. Something surprising about them is that they'll insist that you pay even ten cents you might owe them. In China we'll usually say no need, but Singaporeans will not. I ask them, 'Do you depend on these ten cents for your life?' They'll say, 'Yes, just pay me.'

When COVID-19 situation got serious, they didn't allow us to go out. The locals could ride bikes, they didn't even need to wear masks. But even if we wore the mask, we were not allowed out. We got transported in vans back and forth from the work site. Even now that things have eased up a lot, we still cannot come out. They are just acting as if we are the ones who brought the disease to Singapore.

If you do something wrong, these Singaporeans will tell you off, no matter how close they are to you. It is like this at work. It is also like this at the church. 'You cannot talk nonsense anymore since you joined the religion,' is what they say. 'You cannot wrongly interpret the Bible. St. David didn't say so.'

I defend Jesus when people say bad things about him. I feel Jesus is quite good. What the church teaches is also good. But they want people to quit the party[60]. I find it unnecessary. I'm not a party member. But you can't force people to quit the party.

The church tells us that the party is just an organization. They tell us why the party is not good. I said, 'If it's so bad, then why are people still saying that there is no People's Republic of China without the Party?' There is a sister-in-charge at the church. She's from China, who came to Singapore to accompany her child for his studies. She said, 'Mao Zedong made a God of himself, this is why it's not good.' I said, 'Mao Zedong is the big saviour, this is in the revolutionary song, *The east is read*. If there is no Mao Zedong, maybe you won't exist.' She said this is 'blasphemy'. I said it's not blasphemy. You'd be killed if you said this at Tiananmen. Here then you talk about 'blasphemy!' See how good the communist party has made China to be. You can keep denying. I don't agree. Mao is our greatest man. We cannot talk badly about him even in private. A great man is a great man. In Xi'an, ShanXi, most families still hang Chairman Mao's portrait on the wall. Do you dare to ask them to take it down and throw it away? Never mind, you keep your view. I won't change mine. This is the only unhappiness I have with them.

My wife is a teacher. She is a junior employee, doesn't make much and gets no salary during school holidays. I want to bring her to Singapore to teach. She wanted to wait till my son went to university. I said, 'By then you'll be too old. Do you think Singapore still wants you if you are that old?'

My son was born in the year of the Monkey and he is seventeen now. He has Nephrotic Syndrome. He went through Spinal Puncture and was in ICU for one day and one night. I asked the doctor what his illness was. The doctor said, 'I have done research for ten years and still don't know what it is.' How annoying! We stayed in that hospital for a few weeks, did all the dripping, hormone medicine, etc., and the symptoms kept flaring up. Last year, he had to stop his studies. I thought it's more important that he just lives. Studies, whatsoever, don't matter. Find a light job in the future. That's it.

---

[60] Communist party in China

One of my hometown people, an intern doctor, recommended us to visit a famous TCM[61] doctor, saying there was no hormone in his medicine. I asked him what does hormone mean. He asked me to Baidu[62]. Since then, we have been on this old TCM doctor's medicine costing 2,000 yuan per month. My son looks healthy, no different from a normal person. He's taller than I am. But his condition worsens again whenever we stop the TCM treatment. Strange.

I don't call home much because I feel bad about my son.

Luckily, I have a mistress. We get along well. Whatever I can't tell my wife, I tell her. My wife always argues with me. Headache. She says she has no time. Okay, if you have no time then I will talk to others. This special one has time. Some days we can talk for the whole day. I'm very happy. Haha. We have never met in person. We only got to know each other online this year. You see, I cannot just work, eat, eat, work. I need energy to work. Won't I become numb otherwise?

My lover also has a tough life. Her old man[63] also went overseas. They have financial problems. Sometimes she cries to me. I said don't cry, I have a headache. I said, 'Remember, you have a family, I also have a family. I'll help you within my limits. The limits are that we can't cross the line. Our families are the priority, and I'll help you when I can.' I buy things for her. She's always in Kuaishou and Tiktok. I have no such time. If I have some time I'll watch TV dramas, and sleep a bit.

These are the two women in my life. My mistress. My big wife.

I didn't plan to work here for long. Now I have no other choice because of COVID. Just take it one day at a time. Not planning far.

My truck that is worth hundreds of thousands of yuan is still at home, idling. Maybe I'll do something with it when I go back.

My dad likes to keep all kinds of animals; we have dogs, pigeons, cats and sheep. If nothing works out, then I'll just go back to rear sheep. You walk and the sheep follow you. You stop and the sheep stop. Sigh, so enjoyable. This kind of freedom and joy, I won't exchange with

---

[61] Traditional Chinese Medicine
[62] Chinese search engine
[63] Husband

anything in the world. Someone's got a girl? Someone's got rich? Yeah whatsoever, just go fuck himself.

I'll buy a horse to ride. Sigh, I have been asking around, a horse costs more than 10,000 yuan. Never mind, I'll just ride my broken tricycle. Or I'll let a sheep pull my cart. I will sit in my little cart pulled by a little male sheep. Woohoo!

Our Heads Became Big from Oversleeping during the COVID-lockdown

Zhou Hongxing (China), forty-nine years old, Construction Worker in Singapore

I was born in Shandong. My poor parents struggled to feed us seven siblings. We ate only preserved vegetables. I didn't do well in studies and went to a veterinary school. There, I learned to check the pulse of cows and goats. I tried my new knowledge on myself and guess what, my pulse was racing at 130 per minute. One doctor diagnosed me with malnutrition and low blood pressure—I had been eating only preserved vegetables due to my tight weekly allowance of 5 yuan. Maybe it was not lack of intelligence but the lack of materials that kept me away from universities.

After graduation, I opened a small clinic treating livestock. I also sold animal feed on the side. In 2006, the farming industry faced a big downturn and meat became cheaper than animal feed; farmers killed their pigs at birth because they couldn't afford feeding them. It was heart-breaking to see old farmers come to my clinic, using their shaky hands to take out their rainy-day reserve wrapped in a piece of cloth, to pay me. I couldn't bear this and looked elsewhere for work.

Those days, I was in dire need of money; school fees for my three-year-old daughter, medical bills for my old father, winter heating, and a lot more. Construction work in China was not an option because they didn't have work during winter. After watching a TV advertisement saying 'Make big money in Singapore,' I went to a training school in Nanjing. There, I worked very hard to make up for my lack of experience. I ate instant noodles during lunchtime and practiced my lessons while others rested. I lost five kilograms but I passed the exam and came to Singapore.

My original plan was to work in Singapore for only a few years. But our expenses back home kept going up. It has been fourteen years and I am still here. I worked in one company after another. I have worked as a rebar worker, carpenter, and cement worker. I'm proud of my work. I'm very happy to see buildings rise higher and higher as I work. International school, private bungalows, housing estates all the buildings I built are like my children. I'm proud of how they look. I have also done fogging for three years; the inspectors never found any mosquitoes in my area.

Life here has not been easy. Construction work is dirty and tiring. I struggled in particular to cope with Singapore's hot weather. At night, I woke up, fully drenched in sweat. I bought myself a fan. But it soon went missing. In my dormitory, the guards rummaged through our things and took away anything they pleased citing non-compliance. We used to joke that our dormitory was the second Changi Prison. But these guards had more power than the police. They even took away the hair clippers we had bought to save on the seven dollars that the barber charged us. The guards then fined us fifty Singapore dollars—they surely sided with the salon.

In my early days, the experienced workers bullied us as newcomers but I proved myself quickly because I could read architectural drawings and complete work faster and better than others, especially the Bangladeshi and Indian workers; Chinese brain after all. Nowadays, the boss gives me the drawings, and I lead the 'blackies'[64] at work.

---

[64] An insulting reference to South Asians

Some of them are smart and willing to learn. Some are dimwit and lazy. I get very annoyed when I teach for many days and he still doesn't get it, and yet he is happy. What can you do with such people? You can't beat him either. Therefore, in the construction industry in Singapore, the blackies can never replace us Chinese.

I treat other workers like brothers. Someone borrowed money from me and became incommunicado after he returned to China. I thought never mind, work two more days and the money will be replenished. Maybe he's in a challenging situation or else he would have returned me the money.

Some people are into drinking, gambling, or womanizing. I ask them, 'Have you ever made any money on gambling? Remember the days you lost and went around borrowing money. You look for prostitutes here, but if your wife also finds a man at home, how would you feel?' I can only try to do my part but cannot convince them. People have their own reasons to not care for their family. Some say that I scare them. But the stories are real.

One story I tell is about a worker who committed suicide after being bullied by his supervisor. The company hired a Taoist priest to do some exorcism rituals . . . the supervisor was fired . . . the boy's father came and the matter was settled . . . things just ended without an ending . . . My fellow Shandong people asked to gather and beat that supervisor . . . I said we came here to make money, what's the use if we beat him? No use anymore . . . Nasty supervisors are common. Many Chinese supervisors only take care of their *Lao Xiang*[65] and give others the heaviest work. It's okay. I am used to this kind of unfairness back in China. Where there are people, there's always politics. But when a worker works beyond his capacity, he gets too tired and careless; that's when accidents happen. If I listen to the supervisor I have to bear the consequences. If I don't, I'll get a salary deduction. Where can I seek justice? Many of us complain to the Ministry of Manpower, but they progress slowly, often taking two to three months. Do we have three months? In the end, we are the ones suffering. This indirectly supports the bad companies. We

---

[65] People from the same town or clan

don't hate the companies. We are angry with the government. I use the story of the worker who committed suicide to tell my colleagues that we need to respect ourselves and be strong. If we take our own life as trivial, no one can help us.

Safety measures in Singapore are better than in China, but still, there are deaths at construction sites every year. We can't avoid all accidents. If anything happens to me one day, my family will receive a hefty compensation. They will be happy even without me. But I don't want such a day and act very carefully at work. I tell my colleagues that if you lose your life, your parents won't find money meaningful. Your wife and your children are no longer yours by then.

Once, I went to an area to check mosquitoes. I didn't know that someone was doing demolishing work right above me. They were supposed to put fencing around there but they didn't. A big window fell on my head. I fainted; when I woke up, I was in the hospital. I had lost a lot of blood. I was shivering. Peter, our safety officer, prayed next to my bed. He requested the nurse for a blanket for me. He was one of the kinder Singaporeans.

Many Singaporeans look down upon us and badmouth China. Many Facebook posts are full of bias and hatred towards migrant workers from China. Maybe they have seen bad apples among us and think all Chinese are the same. If I do anything wrong, they will point, 'China, China'. So I am always cautious because I am a representative of my country when outside. I always clean up the site after working; I stay in one remote corner when taking the train wearing sweaty clothes; I give seats to the elderly. I had once wanted to become a soldier. I couldn't become one but I will defend my country on Facebook like a fighter. Even if my mother nation is ugly, other people cannot look down on her. I always defend China saying that my country is not as poor as they think, China will overtake the US as the world's biggest economy and many villagers in China also have houses and cars. I tell people that we Chinese workers have given our best years to Singapore, working hard to build the city while always obeying the law.

Last year, during COVID lockdown, many people insulted us, saying we purposely got ourselves infected to get free government money. They called us lazy and vain. Such comments hurt. Much of the government money didn't reach us. And we wanted to work badly. I was thinking about my work all the time—will that board become rotten, left unattended for so long? I hope people can be more empathetic towards us.

The number of cases in the dormitory was growing so quickly. The government took away many confirmed positive patients from the dormitory, but left their belongings with us. It was hard to avoid contact with those when we moved around. We begged to get tested for COVID. Some doctors came, but they only worked limited hours and had lengthy breaks. One of my roommates was denied a COVID test even when he felt sick, just because his temperature was 0.1 degrees below the minimum requirement to be tested. I told him to squat at the gate, and they finally took him in. One colleague died in the bathroom after recovering from COVID. Another one suddenly collapsed on the ground after a run. COVID had caused blood clots in his head. His surgery failed and he became a vegetable.

On 5 April 2020, the loudspeakers announced that no one would be allowed out of the dormitory (COVID restrictions). We rushed to stock up on rice, oil, and instant noodles. Initially I was happy; I thought I could rest and the government would anyway pay us money. But just a few days later, I found this endless period of rest and restricted movement unbearable. The money also didn't arrive as promised: The companies deducted a large part of the 750 Singapore dollars using all kinds of excuses. I got only 400 dollars in the first month and only 150 in the second. Food came either too early— becoming cold by mealtime—or too late. The rice smelled musty. When asked, the staff said that Singapore's rice imports were affected due to COVID and that this rice came from old stocks. Some churches brought us loads of instant noodles, Lao Gan Ma[66], and eggs. Initially, the guards rejected them on our behalf, saying that we were 'having a good enough life inside'. Later the churches managed to get a special permit and delivered the food to us. We were so grateful. Without them, Singapore's reputation would have further suffered in our hearts.

---

[66] A chili sauce staple from China

No outsider can imagine the mess in our dormitory during those early days of COVID. With over 10,000 people in a closed environment and no cleaner at work due to worsened COVID situation, cleanliness was impossible. Bangladeshis and Indians didn't care about cleanliness, so most confirmed cases were these people, not Chinese. Phlegm, cigarette butts, and other trash were everywhere. I couldn't take it anymore and picked up the fire extinguisher hose to wash the ground. When the guard saw me, he said I deserved a fine for misuse of the hose. I argued that the cleaners had used this water previously. He stopped me but said that he respected me, for out of 10,000 workers, I was the only person who thought of cleaning. The virus wouldn't have spread so much if we had a cleaner environment. The lockdown was not to fight the fire but to keep the burning within closed doors.

We were in lockdown for half a year. We couldn't understand why the government locked us down for so long. We were not animals. Even cats and dogs get a daily walk. I was so envious of the birds: at least they could fly. But the guards kept telling us, 'Sleep, sleep'. Our heads were becoming big because of the excessive sleep.

During the lockdown, my contract was about to end. I wanted to go back to China, but my company refused to buy air tickets even though it was in the contract. While I negotiated with them, they stopped my daily food catering from the government. After having nothing to eat for one full day, I told the officer from the Ministry of Manpower. He seemed surprised and brought me some biscuits. I . . . I said, (sobs) . . . I am not trying to eat your food. Either you let me go back home or allow me to change companies, then I can work and pay for my own food. The officer said that he would help me to solve the problem. With his help, I was taken to a charity organization to be quarantined for fourteen days and then an air ticket was given to me for free. I was probably the only person who got a free ticket. Everyone else I know had to pay by themselves.

I tested positive when I arrived in Shanghai; but I was perfectly fine when leaving Singapore. I was quarantined for sixteen days and recovered soon. I thought I wouldn't return to Singapore. But China was also suffering from COVID, and I couldn't make ends meet with the work there. When my colleagues in Singapore told me about their salary increments, I decided to return.

There are still COVID cases in my dormitory. Now we are very good at testing, whenever someone is still fast asleep in the morning, we know. I was the ninth person in my room to get COVID-19. I actually felt relieved; after many days of worry I could finally take a well-deserved rest. Since I had no symptoms, I was only quarantined for four days. My wife asks me to come back home. I say I don't want to bring this disease to my loved ones. When your clothes catch fire, you don't run home.

I work six days a week and sometimes on Sundays too; I take only three days of holiday during Chinese New Year; I rarely take any sick leave and work even when sick; I send home all my salary, keeping little for myself. I don't drink alcohol, I don't smoke either. I spend only on phone bills, toiletry, and transport. Occasionally I buy a little lottery ticket, but always less than five dollars. My wife complains that after trying so long, I have never won a thing. I just don't have the luck. On weekends, I go to church with friends to enrich my life. I don't have any belief, I am not a communist either. The church is okay, it doesn't teach us to do anything wrong.

I always try to express my love for my family. In video calls, I listen to my wife patiently when she feels hassled. When the weather there turns cold, I buy things like a hand warmer for my child and a thermal blanket for my wife. Sometimes I top-up their phone cards. When my wife wanted to stop paying for heating—it cost 3,000 yuan or 470 US dollars a year—I stopped her from doing so. Working outside, I can afford a better life for my family. After sending money home, I find such joy calling my wife; no word can describe that.

I am going through all my struggles here in order to build my family's better future. But I still feel guilty for not being with them. I feel most guilty to my parents and then to my wife. In these fourteen years, I have only been home for a combined total of two months. But holidays mean salary deduction. My wife's life is not easy. She has to manage all duties to our relatives and help our kid prepare for university exams. She jokes sometimes that I have run away, offloading everything on her shoulders.

My daughter often complains about me. I know the best love for children is companionship. But all I could send home was money. That moment I left home for Singapore the first time, my three-year-old girl was fast asleep. She will be in university soon. I will never have the chance now to be with her in her childhood and youth; this is not something any amount of money can buy. Once, when I couldn't go home for the Mid-Autumn Festival, she cried, 'Other people's parents are all coming back. Will you only come back when my mother dies?'

Before going back home for the first time, I searched hard for a good gift for my daughter. It was not easy because I had so little savings then. After long, I just picked up an abandoned teddy bear next to a dustbin in a housing estate, washed it up, and gave it to her. My daughter loved it so much; she often took it to bed. For her, it was not a toy but love from papa.

No matter what, coming to Singapore was worth it. Our house back home is now fully paid for! We are debt-free. I felt so relieved because of this that I bought a new Huawei phone. If all goes well, I'll only need to fight for a few more years. I'd then be able to get my daughter through university, buy her a house, get her married, and then get her kid into a good kindergarten once she has one. Singaporean parents don't care so much once their children start working. But I must give her the best future. Otherwise, all my suffering will be pointless!

My daughter tops her school. Maybe she can study in Singapore someday. Maybe then our paths will overlap in some way, maybe then this city we would have in common, compensate for all the hugs I couldn't give her when she was a child. Do you know that song? I found it on the internet.

'Is it a hug when I feel the breeze you felt?

Is it being together when I walk the path you walked?'

Working with Chinese Workers

*Md Sharif (Bangladesh), forty-two years old, Safety
Coordinator in Singapore*

For many years, my job was that of a site supervisor or safety officer, working alongside people from various cultures. My observations on their differences are based on this experience.

Around 2013–2014, I was working in the Tuas area as the site-supervisor. Most of the workers there were over 300 Chinese who came from China and the rest, about 100, were Indians and Bangladeshis. It was a multi-storey construction site and I was assigned to supervise the lowest storey. This was challenging because this storey was also serving as the rest area for the workers. The Chinese workers didn't use the assigned rest area only for resting; many would sleep there overnight. But since it was only a rest area, we didn't provision for necessary facilities like toilets or enough space for all. As per rules, they could only eat catered food in the rest area. But the Chinese never followed any rules. They would plug in water kettles and cook their own noodles. Sometimes, they didn't dispose of the noodle-cups and maggots would form inside. The whole area became very smelly. They would plug in so many electric devices that there would be frequent power-trips.

They would smoke illegal cigarettes even though smoking itself was not allowed.

My manager asked me to monitor their behaviour. I tried to explain to the Chinese workers that these things were not allowed. I talked to them nicely. But nothing changed. I had to be sterner and mention fines and penalties. They began ignoring me. They would argue in whatever English they could speak. Maybe not everyone was so unruly. But a few were uncontrollable.

The Chinese workers would often walk around wearing nothing or very little. Many important people used to come to check the site and then they would see people walking around semi-naked, smoking. We felt bad about this; our bosses felt bad. But it was impossible to change their behaviour.

I was stuck in the middle. The managers told me to monitor the Chinese workers but they themselves had some weakness towards them. They just said that the Chinese workers are uncontrollable so you manage them yourself.

The Bangladeshis and Indians don't want to work alongside Chinese workers. The Chinese workers usually do the hardest tasks, like plastering, cementing. The Bangladeshis and Indians are assigned to the Chinese workers as assistants, to help them with the tools. The Chinese work very hard and fast, with intense focus. The Bangladeshis and Indians just can't cope with their speed. They don't have the same physical strength as the Chinese, perhaps because of different food habits. The Chinese work non-stop. The Bangladeshi or Indian likes taking many breaks. Moreover, the Chinese earn a lot more, like 100 Singapore dollars a day; the Bangladeshi or Indian makes only 18–20 Singapore dollars a day. So the Bangladeshi or Indian working alongside the Chinese is already unhappy. If a certain task is given to the workers, the Chinese would try to finish it as fast as he can, say within the normal working hours of nine-five. The Bangladeshi or Indian assisting him then misses out on the overtime payment. The Chinese, on the other hand, are often employed on task-based contracts so they don't care about overtime. All these cause resentment.

But there are many admirable things about the Chinese. He has a certain love, passion and dedication towards work. Any work the company gives him, he thinks it is his own work, not the company's work. They are so focused. Also they don't show-off like the Indians and Bangladeshis. The Indian or Bangladeshi wastes his money on nice phones, nice clothes, and having girlfriends in Singapore. The Chinese don't waste. He is practical. He will have only two sets of T-shirts, two sets of pants, and a towel. Every day, after he finishes his work for the day, he will wash whatever he wore at work so that it's dry for the next day. I like such things about them.

And not that the Indians are without problems. They drink a lot. You will often see them here and there, lying on the floor, on the footpath, in their dormitory, unconscious from heavy drinking. The Chinese also drink a lot; they drink and smoke like we drink water. But they can hold, they don't drop anywhere like the Indians.

But anyone can adjust with anyone once they develop some familiarity. During COVID lockdown, I was in a dormitory with a Chinese worker. There were some other workers too from Bangladesh and India. The Chinese man was old, in his seventies. We all felt rather sad for him. His bunk-bed was in the topmost tier and he would struggle to climb up to it. We offered our beds to him. But he would just smile and decline our offer. We became friends. He shared his Chinese food with us. We shared ours with him. So you can be friends with Chinese workers also if you know them over time. You can then trust each other.

The Only Chinese Worker in an Indian Restaurant

Blissful Life (name changed), China, fifty-eight years old, Cleaner in a Restaurant in Singapore

I come from Sichuan, China. I live in Singapore with my husband who works here as a construction worker. For almost two years, I have been working in an Indian restaurant. The government requires Indian restaurants to have at least one Chinese worker, and I'm that Chinese person for this restaurant. I don't even know the name of the restaurant. I just knew that it is near a shopping mall and a supermarket and how to travel from my rented place.

Working in an Indian restaurant has been okay; but I just can't take their food. I usually have lunch at home before starting work at 1 p.m. For dinner, I don't have a choice but to eat their food. Else I'll have to eat at home very late; only after finishing work at 10 p.m. My boss liked my work very much, but things changed with the arrival of the new manager, a relative of my boss. He complains to the boss about everything I do, no matter how small a thing. The boss does not come over much. Whatever the manager tells him, he believes.

One day, I was washing an enormous cooking pot and some water splashed into my eyes. I couldn't hold on to the cooking pot and bang! It dropped it on the floor. The manager complained to the boss, saying I purposely dropped it to create loud noise and annoy the customers. The boss came and scolded me for my bad attitude. I couldn't explain myself.

I can never defend myself when they talk. I lived in Sichuan for more than fifty years—I don't know English, I don't know any Indian language. This language problem is a big one. The Indians are always talking among themselves. I can't make out what they are saying. I couldn't even read my contract, so someone else explained it to me. Whenever I spot a Chinese-looking customer in the restaurant, I ask them to help me talk to my manager or the boss. A Chinese chef, a Singaporean uncle, and a Chinese girl were among them.

When I get interpretation help from these customers, I try to tell the manager not to inform the boss of everything. I really hate it. We migrant workers should help each other and work in harmony. If there are minor problems, we should sort them out together.

The manager doesn't answer me. Instead he tells these customers all his complaints about me. He says I talk to him rudely; that I call him by pulling his clothes or pinching his arms. He says that we live in civilized Singapore, not China or India and that customers would see us and think badly. But how else can I ask him to come over? He doesn't understand Chinese.

He also complains that I often make loud, shocking noises. I was so angry. Why don't they then come and help me! Three or four of them Indians stand together chatting, not attending to the customers, leaving me, a woman, alone, to wash the heavy pots, each a few kilograms. I have so much work, and still, they all make me clear dishes, so unfair! It's supposed to be shared work!

My agency contract has fifteen days of annual leave and sick leave. I never took any leave and didn't get any money in return. I never knew that I had to be the one to apply for leave; I thought the boss would just tell me when to go on leave. I swear that I will take all my leave during Chinese New Year next time. Now that my contract is due for renewal, I asked the boss about my earlier leaves. The boss became pissed and told me that he would clear all our old accounts.

Things have gotten worse of late. Nowadays, all my four Indian co-workers take turns to find fault in me. They say I clear the customers' plates too quickly, before the customers have even finished eating. How can that be? I have been clearing dishes the same way the last two years, and now I'm suddenly wrong? I know I can't stay here long. The boss hasn't asked me to leave, but I have to look for other jobs. I have contacted my old agent and asked some friends if they had jobs. Nothing useful so far. Now I don't fucking dick care about these people at the restaurant; I will just keep working till they ask me to leave.

Wanting to be Like a Local, But . . .

Anirban (India), twenty-eight years old, Driver, domestic migrant worker in Shillong (North-east India)

I just want to be here. I have got a Meghalaya ID now. I have an Assam ID also. Next year, I will buy-out this car from my boss. Then I can be my own boss. I am saving for that. I like it here. While driving, I meet many new people like you. Back in Assam, it is the same people every day, the same mentality. How can I get in my village what I can get in Shillong? There is no excitement with the people back there, only criticism. Do you want a Meghalaya ID? I can get you in one week. I know important people here, from my driving. I can put in a good word and you will get the ID in three days.

I want to be like a local. I have started eating their food a lot, very different from us Assamese people; (they) eat a lot of meat. I can speak their language also now, more or less I can manage. Of course, I look different but not too different. I almost married a Khasi girl. The Khasis have a different system. Among them, the youngest daughter inherits everything from her family. The husband has to stay in her home and take care of her parents. So all Khasi men want to marry the youngest daughter. I too once dated a Khasi girl who was the youngest daughter. She loved me very much. But when I proposed marriage, she said that I have to change my religion, my surname and that I have

138

to move over to their house. Now tell me why must I do that? Why should it be me to change my surname?

I am married now. Eventually, my parents found a good girl for me from my village in Assam. How could I have married the Khasi girl anyway, with all their conditions? I am a very modern man but I can't lose my prestige completely right? Everyone would have done the same thing, no?

My God or Their Allah, All is the Same

*Arun (India), twenty-eight years old, Marine Worker, was
a domestic migrant worker in India, currently working in
Singapore*

I am not sure about my actual birthday. Parents just wrote a random
date when they put me in school. I was born in a small village in
Jharkhand province, near the border with the province of West Bengal.
The village is very small, very remote. I have a sister and a brother.
I am the eldest. My mother is a homemaker. My father is an itinerant
fish-seller. He would buy 15–20 kg of fish in the big market every day
and then roam around different villages to sell that fish. He is doing
that even today.

You can say that my family's history is quite tragic. My grandfather
died when my father was only thirteen years old. He was the eldest
among five siblings. My grandmother told me that my father had to
stop his own schooling to take care of the whole family. Slowly, bit
by bit, he built some economic stability for the household. He got all
his brothers and sisters married. Today we are doing better, we have
some position in society, some standing; because I work overseas, my
sister is married to someone working overseas, but all this is because
of how my father worked hard and sacrificed his own future to build
something from nothing.

I don't have much education, only till Higher Secondary. I studied for a few years in Jharkhand and then in a school in the nearby village in West Bengal. I did enroll at a university for English Honours but I quit halfway and started working. I was just a nineteen year old boy then. I won't hide why I started working at such a young age. There is no need to be ashamed. It is better to tell the truth, to say exactly what happened. I don't want to show myself in a good light by lying. The issue was love. There was love, there was heartbreak, and then there was an accident. After this accident, my lover died. I mean, she committed suicide because she couldn't handle her depression. What was my age then? Only eighteen. The way I can understand life now, I didn't have that capability back then. At that age people think with their hearts, not their brains. Back then, we just lived for the moment. After this, I was not in a mental position to continue studying. The girl's family was angry. They blamed me for everything. They could have beat me up, or even worse. My family said that it was better for me to leave. So I fled. I ran away, to the other end of India.

I first went to Chhattisgarh, then to Maharashtra, and then to Gujarat. I started working. Couldn't I have gone back to the university? Couldn't I have started my studies again after things settled down a bit? Well, when one starts working, when one starts seeing money in one's hand, it is hard to give it up. Also, I left home with my closest friends. Some more friends joined us later. Once you are among friends, every place becomes familiar, everything becomes enjoyable.

In 2019, I came to Singapore, with the same company that I was working for in India. How did I feel when I first came to Singapore? I can't explain. Feelings can only be felt; they can't be described in words. There is a joy of boarding one's first flight in life. There is a joy of going overseas for the first time. My favourite subject in school was Geography. This love for the subject gave me such an intense desire to travel. But coming from a lower middle-income family, how can one travel, be it inside or outside India? So when I got to know that my company had an office in Singapore, I was hoping that they would send me here someday. I believe that if someone really wants something, it happens. In my case, it did happen, right? But I must say that this doesn't mean that I don't love my own country. My only reason for coming to Singapore is that here I can earn a lot more for the same work. That is the unfortunate truth of my country. There is nothing to sugar-coat about it.

I love travelling. I have always loved. But in my two years in Singapore, I have hardly seen anything. Only sometimes, when my company takes me in a boat to the worksite, I can catch a glimpse of famous buildings like what's the name of that one . . . Marina Bay Sands? Yes. Okay, Sundays are a holiday. But we have come to Singapore only to make money. This is always running in my head. So I am always hoping to get work, even on Sundays, just so that I can earn that little extra. Only if that is not possible, I take some rest. Some of those times, I go out with my friends, that too only nearby. At the very least, I want to see the INA[67] Memorial once. I am a huge fan of Subhash Chandra Bose, our national hero and leader of the INA. While being in Singapore, if I don't see the INA memorial at least once, it would be very pitiful indeed.

In Singapore, I do the same work as I did in my first job. I have always worked in the marine sector, with heat treatment for welding. There is no education or training for my line of work. What you do is just what you learn on the job. There is no certificate that one can get. At best, you can get a written letter from your company saying that you have been a good worker. My job has two safety risks. We work with live power and anything with live power carries risks. But there are many safeguards for that and unless one is really unlucky, bad things don't happen. The second risk comes from inhaling the powdered glass that is used for insulation. The powdered glass can be used at most twice when we do the welding. But sometimes the company wants to save money; it pressurizes you to use it more than twice. If this happens, say not just once or twice but if it happens daily, then the dust from the powdered glass accumulates in the lungs and you can get tuberculosis. Maybe there are other long term effects also. Some of us, those who have been doing this for twenty-thirty years,

---

[67] Indian National Army

have their own remedies for this. They say, 'Eat bananas or jaggery daily, these foods trap the dust, then you won't have any problem'. Who knows? I don't think there is any scientific evidence. But I wear a N95 mask when working. I have been doing this since 2012; ten years and nothing has happened. What does that say? That says that if you follow proper procedures, you can even do dangerous things. I don't eat any bananas. I don't have much interest in fruits. To tell you the truth, during COVID lockdown, the government gave us bananas and lemon every day. I never even touched those.

I have been a migrant worker in India. I am now a migrant worker in Singapore. 90 per cent, there is no difference. I am doing the same work, there or here. I had to work alongside strangers in India. I have to work with strangers in Singapore as well; well, slightly different kinds of strangers. Where I live is similar as well. In places where I worked in India, three or four of us shared one room, within the worksite. But there we had cooks to prepare our food. It is almost the same in Singapore, just more people in one dormitory room that is also very close to my worksite. But here, I have to cook. I don't like to eat in restaurants. Once in a while, it is okay to eat outside, just for a change of taste. But I like my own cooking. So it is okay. But there is one big difference. In India, if I don't like the job or face any issue, I can just leave. I can just pack up and go back home. Someway or the other, I can escape. But I can't leave Singapore on a whim. The implications are far more. Also I have to follow a certain process. During August last year—the corona period—I wanted to go back home. But it was not so easy. There are not as many options. I couldn't go. That is a big difference between working here versus working in India as a migrant worker. Also the way the family communicates with you is different. When you are overseas, they say since you are overseas, it is okay, arrangements must be good there. But if I am in India, they will be like, 'No need to struggle there son, just come back home, it is not worth it'.

I can't complain about my life in Singapore. I knew exactly what it would be like when I signed the contract. Moreover, my personality is such that I can adjust to any condition, no matter how bad it is.

I can adjust even with the worst human beings. So I have never had any problems anywhere. I am a peace-loving person. I don't like to get into arguments. Only once, when I was a kid, I had a big fight with a friend. So I still remember it so vividly. In my dormitory room here, there are three Bangladeshis and a few Indians, from Tamil Nadu, Himachal Pradesh, Andhra Pradesh and Bihar. As I told you, I mould myself into any circumstance. Let's talk about religious or language differences. Even though I don't consider myself as particularly religious, I am still a practicing Hindu. So I do my religious duties inside our room, like performing evening prayers. In the same room, we have Bangladeshi Muslims who pray five times a day in their style. I don't have any problem with that. My God or their Allah, all is the same. As long as we understand this, we can live together. And I am someone who is mild-mannered. Before reacting to anything, I think twice. But I must say that many Bangladeshis do have an anti-Indian sentiment. Similarly, many Indians have an anti-Bangladeshi sentiment. This can't be ignored, especially in my case. I consider myself a Bengali with all my heart, mind and soul, even though I was not born in West Bengal or Bangladesh. In Singapore, many get surprised to hear that I am a Bengali but that I am not from Bangladesh. They don't know that there are so many Bengalis in India. They ask me why am I not a Muslim? Why don't I eat food like theirs, this and that? But I don't care. Language is just a matter of identity. The way someone treats me, I treat that person the same way, whatever his identity. Now let's talk about food. In our room, different groups of people form their own groups for cooking. The Bangladeshis cook and eat together. I cook with two other roommates who come from South India. I am okay to eat whatever they cook as per their cuisine. They eat more sour-sour food, using a lot of tamarind. I am fine with that. When I feel like having something from my own cuisine, I just tell them, 'Brothers, let me be the one to cook today'.

I have great respect for the directness and simplicity of Singaporeans. I have my own experiences. I have to wear safety shoes which have to be zipped up. Sometimes, I just don't zip it up. One Singaporean in the workplace noticed this. He was observing me for a while.

Then he came up to me and said gently, 'Brother, zip up. Else you may slip and get hurt'. It was so nice of him. Or when you go to a shop or to a restaurant or canteen, when you give them money, their style of taking it respectfully with two hands and giving you the change back with two hands while bowing to you gently, all these manners are really praiseworthy. Or their civility, like when you are queuing for tea or coffee at a shop, they don't overtake you but ask first whether you are queuing. I haven't faced any discrimination or rude behaviour myself so I can't talk about it.

During the early days of COVID-19, it was very tough for migrant workers. But I didn't feel terrible because everything that was happening to me was happening to all other migrant workers. Was I alone in my suffering? No. The way Singapore managed it, the way they arranged for our food, all of that is praiseworthy. Of course, the food might not have tasted the best—that depends on a person's taste—but at least the government thought about us, that's what matters. I got infected in April 2020. Everyone in my dormitory room was infected. But the way the containment facility welcomed us like guests, the way they arranged for entertainment and everything for us, I didn't feel like a patient at all, I felt like a hotel guest. So all this gave me courage. It gave me confidence. And when one is courageous and confident, no disease or virus can beat him. So there is a certain trust I have in Singapore because of the way I saw them managing COVID-19. I am sure now that however bad things get, somehow the country will take care of us.

My family is pressuring me to get married. I don't want to. There is a different joy in being single. There are no restraints, except for a few chains from one's parents. I think my character is like a bohemian, like a vagabond. So I find it difficult to settle down. I don't like interference in my life from anyone. I don't like anyone saying things like why are you staying in a dormitory, why do you live like this? But the family thinks differently. They are old fashioned in their thinking. I have had heated arguments with them about this. Maybe I will have to relent. But I won't get married to someone I don't agree with. I have at least that much sense of responsibility. Of course, I have had an incident before. My family is still worried about that. Earlier, I used to roam around a lot; I would hang out with friends, sing. I would return home very late at night. When I go back home now, my family doesn't allow me to do that anymore. I have lost that freedom. I have lost the arguments to argue with them. But what has happened has happened. If something worse is in store, I just have to face it.

I love reading motivational books, like the ones by Swami Vivekananda. At home, we have books like the Geeta and Ramayana. My father forces me to read them whether I want to or not. I wouldn't say that I don't want to read these books. I read the Geeta once and I felt a lot more mature after that. My father says, 'Whether you like it or not, one must eat teeta[68], and whether you understand or not, you must read the Geeta. Just keep reading and automatically something will come inside you.'

I try to be happy with small things. I don't measure my memories like this was the best or that was the worst. Whatever happens, I try to maintain balance. The saddest times were perhaps during COVID's early days. But that was for everyone, not just for me so why complain? As for happy memories, I remember the changes of weather back home, how the *Shiuli*[69] flower bloomed in winter. Here, everything is artificial. But in my native village, there is a certain charm. When I go back home, I just take a mat and sit under a banyan tree near a pond. Staying there under the tree, near the village pond, the air feels different. Time just goes by. Back home, my skin turns darker because I am less indoors. Of course, there is less development. There is no electricity at times. But I have my mobile. I can get entertained wherever I am. I don't need an uninterrupted power supply for TV and all that.

Then there is a pain of staying away from home, from family, for so long. Every day I talk for so long to my mother, it is a different kind of longing and attachment. It would be so much nicer to be staying close to my family. It would be so much nicer if I could just work somewhere nearby and come back home every day. There was some hope. There was a rumour; that a new power plant will be built in my area. Maybe I could get work there, if not at the plant itself then

---

[68] Bitter things
[69] Night-jasmine

I could just start a small shop in that area because when economic development happens, many other opportunities arise. But till such things happen, I will just have to work here. I am not saying that I hate my job. If I really hated my job then it would have been impossible to continue. But what I am doing here are not the things I was passionate about. My passion was singing, literature, and teaching. I loved singing. I still do. Right now as I am talking to you about music, I get a different excitement; see I am getting goosebumps. I love songs for their lyrics. As Abdul Kalam[70] said, 'When you are happy, feel the music, when you are sad, feel its lyrics'. And I was teaching younger children even when I was a student myself. I was so influenced by my teachers that just like them, I hoped that I could be a positive influence on younger kids from my village. But none of that could happen. I can no longer do what I was passionate about. Those dreams, I can't fulfill them as dreams anymore. Now, I can only practice them as a hobby. Even that too is uncertain. So my best outcome is that at least my dreams become my hobbies.

[70] Former President of India

Part VI

How does migration affect the personality and outlook of a person? Does he or she become more progressive? Do they become more religious in order to cope with the unfamiliarity of their new lives? Do they appreciate their home more? Or do they feel that their home has now become an alien world? Do they even want to go back?

In this section, the featured migrant workers—Salman Brischik, A.K. Zilani (Bangladesh); Rajendra (Nepal); Eli Nur Fadilah, Yuli Riswati, Figo Kurniawan (Indonesia); R Vijayakanth (India)—dwell on these questions and more as they narrate their life stories.

I Remember Everything

Salman Brischik (Pseudonym), Bangladesh, twenty-nine years old, worked in various jobs in Malaysia

I was born in a small village near Rangamati, in the hilly part of Bangladesh. We are two brothers and two sisters. My father worked in the army. My mother is a homemaker.

I was a very naughty child. Often I stole the boats of the fishermen in our area. I would take one boat and roam around the lake the whole day. Often I skipped school. I would leave home saying that I was going to school but would actually roam around. My mother scolded me a lot for these things.

I had difficulty adjusting when we moved to a bigger village. I started keeping to myself. I spent a lot of time just looking at the hills and rivers there.

My father enrolled me in the army college. He wanted me to join the army. I didn't like it there. I am a person who loves freedom. I couldn't adjust to the tough discipline in that college.

After completing college, I joined Chittagong University. I loved the university campus. There were many hills and a beautiful lake. Every day, I took my diary and sat by the lake to write. But my writing also got me involved in university politics. That made life difficult for me because of the way political gangs work in Bangladesh. I was living in an atmosphere of fear. It became impossible to continue. So I applied to universities overseas and got calls from Malaysia and New Zealand. We didn't have enough money for New Zealand. So I spent 170,000 taka to join the Multimedia University in Melaka in Malaysia. I arrived there in 2015.

I liked Melaka. I loved the river there. At first, I had challenges in adjusting with the other students. They were from China, from South Africa. But later, I began enjoying their company.

After six months, my family faced a financial crisis. So they said that you have to start earning. So I left Melaka and came to Kuala Lumpur, almost impulsively. In KL, a friend of mine was working in a fish store. He got me a job there. I could make 40,000 to 45,000 taka a month. The money was not bad. But soon I began questioning my decision. I had never done such work before. It was hard. The trucks brought in up to 150 kg of fish. My job was loading, unloading and moving those heavy boxes. I had to work from eight in the morning till seven to 7.30 in the night. I had never worked so hard before.

I was not happy at that place. But I was forced to continue because of my family situation. The company changed my tasks frequently. It always involved heavy lifting but sometimes I was put in the vegetable department, then in the biscuits and snacks department and then in the fish department. I couldn't understand my tasks very well because of so many changes. So they used to talk to me harshly. In particular, I had a lot of difficulties with the Tamil men. The Tamil women, on the other hand, are very hardworking; I had many friends among them. The Tamil men, though, think that they are gangsters. They were very aggressive. Just the way they spoke, the way they called me, the way they scolded me for any mistake I made, I found them very rude. I think the Tamils didn't like me because of my skin colour. They used to ask me, 'All you Bangladeshis are dark, why are you light skinned?' I think they couldn't accept it. I told one that my parents came from Pakistan, that's why. One day, one Tamil man dumped a lot of garbage in my work area. When I complained, he threatened to hit me. I said if you want to fight, then go ahead, but the CCTV will see what happened, who started all this.

My physique changed with all this lifting. I was no longer the skinny student. I was now a muscular labourer. And I slept very well. Whether I was happy or not, the work was so tough that at night, the moment I hit my bed, I would be fast asleep. I would plan to play with my phone but no, it would just fall out of my hands as I crashed.

The company had put me up in the worker's accommodation just above the store. There were three rooms, two toilets and one kitchen. For some reason, they just made me sleep on the floor in the walkway. People walked past me all the time. After one month, the boss let me move into one of the rooms. I shared this room with seven other migrant workers, all from Bangladesh, some from my own district. They assigned some household chores to me. The days when it was my turn, I had to wake up really early in the morning to cook the rice for all. I had to also help with preparing ingredients for dinner. I had difficulty adjusting with them. I was new while the others had been there from before. They would always pick issues with my work.

After six months, I started liking the job. I understood my tasks better. I was now self-sufficient; I felt a certain pride in that. My supervisor also started liking me. I could now get along with others, the Chinese, the Malays, even the Tamils. The Tamils would even bring food for me from home. By now, I too talked like the Tamil men, very aggressively.

I became especially close to one Tamil girl. She worked in my department. At first, she was rather rude. But all of a sudden, she changed. One day, my supervisor asked me to load and unload a lot of cartons. It was hard and tiring. I got very angry. I was not arrogant but just surprised how humans in a developed country like Malaysia could be asked to do such work. Then this Tamil girl took pity on me and asked me nicely if I had eaten my lunch. A few days later—it was the day after Hari Raya—she came in a bike and shouted for me to come out of my room and join her for a ride around town or go for a movie. I asked her why she was behaving like this with me. She said that she realized that she hadn't been fair to me. I asked whether the Tamil men would beat me if they saw us like this. She said she would take care of them. So we became very close friends. Once, we even went to the Cameron Highlands together. She shared all her marital issues with me. But once, she also invited me home for her wedding anniversary.

Thus one day became two days and then three; time passed by. I got along with everyone at the store, except for my fellow Bangladeshis, the people from my same district. There was so much jealousy and politics among them. If the boss spoke to me nicely, they would get jealous and complain. Around then, one of the senior workers left. He was the only one who had a full room all to himself. Since my boss had started liking me by now, he gave me his responsibilities, and also that room. I had this room all to myself now. The other Bangladeshi workers were so jealous. They began saying so many things against me. I told them that I have nothing to do with you all. I stopped having dinner with them.

After work, I began eating at Malay, Chinese and Indonesian restaurants. At these places, I talked to other migrant workers from various countries. I became friends with them. I began understanding their problems. There was one construction worker from Indonesia who offered me cigarettes. He said that he was stuck forever in this life as a migrant worker. His passport and visa had expired long ago. He didn't know how to get it renewed without getting caught. The employer knew this and paid him less. Even my employer had many illegal workers so they could pay less. They love this situation. The Indonesian man said that his condition was hopeless. But when he called home, he would say that everything was fine. All migrant workers were like him. We had many problems. But when we called home, we just said that all was fine.

What I liked about Malaysia was that it changed me. I got exposed to so many cultures. I tried to learn something from each. A Bengali remains a Bengali wherever he goes. He will keep wanting rice and curry. I am also like that. But I could start loving Chinese food, Indonesian food, or Indian food. I didn't like Malay food because they add so much sugar to their food, very different from us Bengalis who like salty and spicy food. Over time I stopped eating Bangladeshi food. My Chinese boss asked, 'What happened?' I said I have become a 'full Chinese'.

As time went by, my student visa expired. I continued working. I was now an illegal worker.

I got harassed by the police a few times. When the police came, the employer just asked us illegal workers to disappear somewhere. That's why illegals just don't step out of their workplace and room. We remain confined to that one building for our entire stay. We remain very fearful all the time. But I didn't want to live like that. I used to go out.

Once the police caught me on the train and asked if I had drugs. I voluntarily opened my bag and spread all the contents on the floor. They let me go. I was not fearful like others. In Malaysia, most migrant workers get harassed anyway. Whether you have the right documents or not, the officials will ask you for 50 ringgit every time they catch you, no matter what.

One day I took a train to KLCC[71] in downtown Kuala Lumpur. Once I got off, a policeman came to me and asked for my documents. He asked why I was in KL and not in Melaka. He put handcuffs on me. Then they took me away in a van. There were other migrant workers inside. I was released after a few hours because I didn't admit that I was working. I kept saying that I was a student who had come to meet friends. But they treated other migrant workers very badly. They scolded them and even beat some. That day I met a Malaysian friend later. I suddenly blurted out to her, 'I don't want to stay in your country anymore'. She asked, 'Why?' I said that people like us come with so many dreams and hopes but all we get is harassment. Nobody helped us, not even our own embassy, no one cared.

After a year and a half, my family's financial situation improved. So I tried to go back to my university. But this time, the school demanded a lot of money. So I started working again, first at a bar and then at a Bangladeshi restaurant. I felt bad. I had come to study and not to work like this. I had also lost the opportunity to make a decent living in Bangladesh. I had spoiled my life. I was funding my brother's education and today he has a professional life. But I don't have a professional life myself. None of my dreams materialized.

---

[71] Multi-purpose development area in Kuala Lumpur comprising of malls, parks and high-rises

Around 2019, a transgender person began harassing me. He used to live in the same building where I was staying. He was a local. He began threatening me saying that if I didn't fulfil his desires, he would report me. I was miserable. That year, I came back to Bangladesh.

I don't think I can work in Bangladesh. In Malaysia or elsewhere, you work hard and you get paid say 50 ringgit a day. But in Bangladesh, to work for a daily salary of 20 ringgit, you have to first spend 1,000 ringgit on bribes or other procedural matters. There's so much corruption, so much bureaucracy. So when I came back, I did nothing for one year. I went back to our house in the village to live with my grandparents. I became like a monk. I lost connection with the whole world. I hardly interacted with anyone. I just spent time with nature and helped my grandmother with some housework. There was a place that I liked a lot during my childhood. This was the Hindu cemetery near the river. When I was a kid, a big river called Nalua used to pass by it. Now, because of climate change, it has dried up and so I call it the Nalua drain, not Nalua River. No one goes there after dark. I went there every day and sat by the banks all day. My hair and beard grew long. I became a wild person.

Sitting by the river, thinking all day for one year, eventually my mindset changed. I decided to do something with my life. I started working as a day labourer for the prawn fishermen in the village. We began at seven in the morning and worked till noon. I helped them with laying nets and sorting the catch. They used to pay me 400–500 taka a day. But I enjoyed working with the fisherman. They were very friendly and had a great sense of humour. The prawns attacked their hands with all its legs so the hands of this fisherman were always bloodied. But they used to make fun of that saying the prawns deserved to avenge their death. I became more interested in life. So I came back to my parents. I came back to the big town.

Nowadays, I work with some newspapers every now and then. Sometimes, I play with a music band and make YouTube videos. Today my brother is working in Malaysia as a marine engineer. That helps the family financially. So I can do what I feel like. At times, my family encourages me, especially my mother, but sometimes they have problems with my current situation, especially my father. Fathers are like that, they worry about the future. Mothers are different. They just want their children to be happy.

All my memories in Malaysia, especially from the early days of my work life there, I keep thinking of them. I remember the hardship. But I also remember the times when I began to have some understanding with the people there. I think of the friends I had made there, the Tamil girl, the Indonesian man. I particularly think of a Nepali boy. He was once working with me in a restaurant. We had become really good friends. The Bangladeshi workers there used to ask me why I preferred him to my own countrymen. I told the Bangladeshis, 'Did you just hear the way you talked? That Nepali man doesn't talk like you all do. That's why.' My friend got involved with an Indonesian girl and one day he took her to his room. Some other Nepali men—his friends— were there as well. They drank a lot of alcohol and then they had a fight over the girl. One of the men stabbed my friend. The next day my boss told me that he was dead. I remember his face every day. I remember everything about Malaysia.

Why is it Wrong to Fall in Love?

Eli Nur Fadilah (Indonesia), twenty-nine years old, Domestic Worker in Singapore

I want to tell the story of how I survived, and how I made people who know me, feel proud of me. I'm proud of myself for surviving without a husband. I sacrifice for my loved ones. I work hard for myself and still enjoy life.

I was born in a small village in Central Java, a decent place with good roads, cars, and motorbikes. I was just unfortunate to have come to this world late—my father died when I had just started going to primary school. Though I had loving brothers, sometimes I felt being treated unfairly. My four older brothers got new bikes from my dad. I, on the other hand, had to rely on government subsidies for school fees and textbooks.

My family was not rich but my family was full of love. My mum was a religion teacher. We were well respected; other villagers sought our advice when they had problems. Even today, people gift us lamb during Hari Raya. My father used to buy fruits from the tree-owners and then sell them in the market. When he went up the tree to pluck the fruits, my mum and I waited below. When we went around villages selling those fruits, my mother held my hand while carrying the basket of fruits on her back; my best memories in life.

With support from my cousins, I completed secondary school and a caregiver course thereafter. At sixteen, I went to Jakarta and began working as a domestic worker. I worked in three different families one after another, each for a very short time. As a teenager, I sought freedom and wanted to be with other young people. Eventually, I went to work in a small café, and then in a minimart.

I came to know a man through a radio dating hotline. He was studying in college. Being all alone in Jakarta, a strange place, my heart needed someone. At eighteen, I got pregnant by him.

My mum asked him to come to our village. She wanted to show people that my child's father was willing to be responsible for my pregnancy. He didn't come. He left me saying he would come back, but he never did; I'm not sure whether he wanted to run away from me or my pregnancy. I do not blame him. I was also responsible since we were both in love.

The situation was more heart-breaking for my mum than me: I could still avoid people by hiding in the house during my pregnancy, but my mum, who was then running a little shop with my brother, had to face people's judgement and questions. I know what society thought of her, like, 'You are a sinner', 'You are a religion teacher, yet you have a grandchild out of wedlock'.

But my daughter didn't choose to be born. I'm the mother who decided to bring her into this world. I don't care about people's judgement.

When my daughter was five months old, I went to another island to work. But the money was not enough for my family. So I moved to Singapore and have been working here since then. Living in Singapore is a luxury for me; I have a room to myself; I get a salary every month; I can eat whatever I want; my work is like living in my own house.

But it was not easy. During my first week in Singapore, I stayed in the employment agency's facility. The agent took me to a prospective employer's house. The Indonesian domestic worker there was crying. The employer was angry. My agent scolded her for crying in front of me, asking her to go into the bathroom. I felt sad and scared.

Eventually, I was placed with an Indian family. I had difficulty adjusting to their food. I had no off-day in the first two years. There were only two bedrooms in the house, and I slept in their boy's room. The boy was in primary school back then. I used to get up at 5 a.m. and prepare three different lunch boxes. Sometimes I felt exhausted. But when I look back, the experience taught me discipline—to live by a timetable.

After two years, I had two half off-days every month. On those days, I attended courses on baking and entrepreneurship. My employer supported my education and paid for these courses. I chose these courses because I wanted to run a bakery. Unfortunately everyone in Indonesia now runs a bakery; the competition is so fierce. They are well funded while I have no savings.

I worked at my first employer's house for five years. Their boy had grown up by then and they didn't need me anymore. For my current employer, I take care of their two teenage kids. The parents had been away for business in Indonesia until recently. When they were not here, I managed the entire household; all the expenses, the kids, the dogs, the grocery shopping, breakfast, dinner—everything. It was perhaps a little too much to expect. Sometimes I felt like the owner of the house, except that I didn't have the money. This experience taught me another lesson—independence. My employer gave me a budget of 200 Singapore dollars. It was often tricky . . . managing three people for three weeks within that sum. I became skilled at budgeting and managing finances.

For my own money, I work, I send, I spend. Finished (money). With whatever is left with me after sending home, I just spend it all away. I have no savings. I know I have responsibility. But I also deserve to enjoy the fruits of my hard work. The most I spent on myself was on the teeth alignment. My teeth have hurt my confidence since I was young. So, I saved and asked my employer to pay my salary in advance. It cost about 2,000 Singapore dollars.

Whenever I send money to my mum, I tell her that it is for her to spend on whatever she likes. Yet, she always reports to me about where she used it. She always tells me that it's **my** money. My principle is 'we earn what we eat'. As long as my family has enough to eat with what we earn, it's good enough. We will be fine so long as we do not copy others and live beyond our means.

My mother is everything for me. She is my role model: for being a woman, mother, and wife. She never relied on anyone. Even when my dad was around, she worked hard. When my dad went to the fields, she woke up early to cook for him. She went to the field with him and still finished all household chores. She speaks up when something is not right. I remember my mum the most for her storytelling. When I was a kid, mum would tell me bedtime stories. You cannot find her stories in any book; they are from her imagination. I used to feel uncomfortable about my body parts, like 'Mom, why do I have such big (fat) legs?' She had a story that went, 'Don't you know, once upon a time, there was a princess who had a big leg'. So beautiful . . . that's how she made me confident, with a tale out of nowhere. Now I think my legs are pretty even if they are chubby. She told us stories of brothers and sisters. Those stories made us siblings, including our step-brothers from my dad's deceased wife, stay together. It's amazing how she could stitch good advice into fairy tales.

My mother is also the reason why I feel marriage is unnecessary. My brothers and my mom still treat me the same way as when I was young. They always make me feel like I'm still a child. Also I have seen many failed marriages. Cheating and divorce is so common. A cousin of mine, married to her childhood love for twenty-five years, has divorced. Her ex-husband married their neighbour, and she went to work in Taiwan as a domestic worker.

Still, sometimes I feel like I need someone to talk to. It's not easy because I need this person to have the same mindset about life. Traditional men think like 'You are my wife; you should stay at home, do housework and serve me'. Marriage should be more than that. I have seen how my parents sacrificed for each other, not making one person do all the work. If there's someone who can treat me the way my dad treated my mum, then yes. He also can't be too traditional. We, women, have our own minds, habits, and the cultures where we grew up in. Men have to respect that.

In any case, it's difficult for us domestic workers to find love in Singapore. You can't marry on the work pass. You get regularly checked for pregnancy by the Ministry of Manpower. They will send you back if you are pregnant or have HIV. There are also many stereotypes against us finding a partner. If you are a FDW[72], and you have a Bangladeshi or Indian construction worker as a boyfriend, it means you crave the weekend sex. And if you date a Singaporean man, you will be seen as a cheap sex object.

Sometimes I wonder: falling in love is human rights, then why is it so wrong to fall for foreign guys?

Some men also take advantage of FDWs. Most of us come overseas with a heavy heart, making us vulnerable and easy to approach. When a guy says, 'I love you,' we melt, give out everything, and lose.

I was well protected by my previous employer so no one could get close to me. My current employer gives me more freedom, which means that I have to take responsibility for my own life and do the right things.

Even then, I've tried but have never succeeded in finding love in Singapore. I have tried to be less judgmental towards men. I had a long-distance relationship with a guy in Indonesia. In the end, he married another lady. So yeah . . . It's not that easy. When someone gets close to me, I like to be straightforward. Do you want to marry me? When? Do you want to know me? Okay, let's talk to my brothers. Do you want to talk to my mother? I'm going back next year, will you come with me? I don't want to waste my time. Maybe this scares the guys.

Maybe I'm still waiting for my ex-boyfriend. He promised to come back to me. It feels like whenever I want to step forward, my past holds back one leg of mine.

I'm not very religious. I don't pray five times a day, but I recite a few prayers before I get out of the house. I used to wear the hijab; and now I don't wear it anymore. I just want to give attention to the most essential things: myself and my happiness. I don't want to focus on rules like 'perhaps I need to cover my hair'. Earlier this year, my friends also advised me that I am prettier without the hijab. I'm the kind of person who listens to other people. Like I'd ask my friends about my outfit before I go out and change accordingly. Yet I respect how my

---

[72] Foreign Domestic Worker

mom raised me and I believe in God. I know when I sleep, my mom prays for me. She wakes up in the middle of the night and has a heart-to-heart talk with the Creator of Life, 'I wish you protect my daughter every day'. Her prayer is my armour, my protection.

I'm not very confident or firm in my convictions. I just told you that I don't feel like wearing the hijab anymore. Still, I have doubts. What will my daughter think of me if I don't? How do I explain? Will people pass their judgment on me?

When my daughter grows up, I hope that she can be happy with her choices, and be courageous to pursue her dreams. Sometimes, she asks me why other kids have a father while she doesn't. I can't breathe when I hear that. I have never told her the truth. Maybe one day I will, when she's ready. She may get angry or feel pain.

Dreams are expensive. Dreams come with big price tags. I had a lot of dreams which changed over time. My dream used to be to make others around me smile. My mom says that when she was exhausted, I was the one to cheer her up. When I was in primary six, I dreamed of being a chef. I knew it would cost 60 million rupiah. If I wanted to be a doctor, I needed 100 million rupiah.

I used to be very active, wanting to do many things, wanting to change the world . . . Now, I only want to cry. Every day, I just wake up, work, watch YouTube; nothing else. I'm just taking a break to focus on myself. I didn't cry much when I left my five-month-old daughter behind. My mum and I didn't even shed a tear when my dad passed away. We are tough. We are strong. But now, sometimes, we cry for no reason.

I went for free counselling for domestic workers. The therapist did hypnotherapy for me. She made me go back to my past, and I met my dad. I cried a lot . . .

Last year, my mother got into depression. This may have to do with her old age, my increasingly rebellious daughter, the death of one of my brothers, or the motorbike accident from which she fractured her hand. The doctor said that she has always had depression because of me having a daughter out of wedlock. Whatever it is, I really need to be with her. My biggest fear is to lose her when I'm not ready.

But I can't go back. My brothers keep begging me to go back. I say, 'Please wait. Bear with it a little.' Going back is like suicide now. I have very little savings. It can last only two-three months. And if I go back, there's no guarantee that I can come back to Singapore. It's exhausting. So many things happened at home, and yet I cannot move. I need to go back next year! I have to, for my mum.

I cannot dream anymore now . . . I'm scared to dream . . . I don't have any dreams for myself . . . Dreams are expensive. But if I'm free to dream, I want to build a shelter for homeless kids. I will change the society around my place, make the mothers work and give them something to think about, not something to talk about, and educate the husbands to not depend on their wives who work overseas.

They Want Someone Smart with Working, but not Smart with Thinking

Yuli Riswati (Indonesia), forty years old, former Domestic Worker in Hong Kong

I was born as the only child in a poor family in East Java, Indonesia. We were farmers without land. My parents were killed in a road accident when I was still a baby. My grandma raised me all by herself.

When I finished elementary school, grandma said that it was enough. My friends could go to high school in nearby cities. Just because I was born as a woman and I had no parents, I had to stick to my village. Such injustice! I had many dreams. I dreamed of getting higher education and a good job, maybe as a teacher. I dreamed of traveling to places I saw on TV to learn more about the world.

Still, I had to listen to my grandma. She was the only person I had and I didn't want to upset her. I also didn't know how to speak up for my dreams. After dropping out of school, I began helping grandma at home and on the farm.

My grandma's biggest worry was that once she passed away no one would take care of me. She believed that only husbands could take care of women. So she found me a husband.

After getting married, I gave birth to a boy. When my son turned two, I asked my husband if I could look for work in another country.

165

At first, my husband didn't agree. I explained to him that I wanted a better future for us. I wanted my boy to be able to go to high school. I didn't want him to become a poor farmer, stuck in a small village. I told him that I was not happy. Being a good wife at home was not meaningful enough. Eventually, he let me go and I found work as a domestic worker in Hong Kong.

I landed in Hong Kong in winter. I had never experienced winter in tropical Indonesia. Oh my God, it was so cold! I found everything so shocking: the jungle of buildings and people, the transportation system, the language . . . But I was very happy. A door to new experiences had finally opened for me.

Before coming to Hong Kong, I had worked hard to learn Cantonese and English at the training centre. But the vocabulary used in my employer's household was very different from what I had learned. I could understand only 30 per cent of what they said. Maybe because of this, my first employer gave me a very low salary. They promised to teach me but gave up within just one week and sent me back to the employment agency.

I was transferred to a new employer. The Sir was jobless; he stayed at home all the time. My Ma'am was always away, working in her office. I took care of their newborn baby and a dog. I had no experience with dogs so it was really hard for me. Once, when the dog was disturbing the baby, my Sir said to me, 'Gaau Doi!' I thought he wanted plastic bag and went to get him one from the kitchen. He became very angry, threw away the bag, went into his bedroom, and banged the door shut. Later, when I told Ma'am about the incident, she laughed a lot and told me that 'Gaau Doi' also meant 'reason'; Sir was actually asking me the reason for all the commotion.

Communication is more than just language. It is also about culture. We Indonesians are taught to avoid eye contact and look down to show respect. When I practiced this in Hong Kong, my employers became angry. They said that I lacked respect because I didn't even look at them when they talked.

Because of such challenges, I always felt stressed. All I wanted was to work and make some money. I began to miss my family, my country . . . In Hong Kong I had no friends, nothing . . . I had no choice but to help myself.

On my off days, I borrowed English books from the library, even though I didn't know English. Learning came naturally to me. Seeing how hard I was trying, my Ma'am allowed me to watch TV with her baby. She asked me to write down the words I didn't understand, and she explained to me when she returned home. Even though this employer paid below minimum wage, I'm grateful that they taught me Cantonese. I only realized how big my vocabulary had become when I met other domestic workers, most of whom only knew words related to food items.

Yet, I was not very lucky in Hong Kong. My employer changed many times. Every employer could be very different. No matter how many years we have worked, having a new employer means that we have to start all over again from zero. To gain our employer's trust is always the toughest. I know that it is also hard for employers to have a stranger in their home. On our side, we tend to have a lot of love for our employer's family even if it's just an employment contract. We feel sad when leaving them, especially the children we took care of. But maybe the employers don't feel the same way; to them, I am just a maid.

I had my first off-day in Hong Kong only after I had worked for several years and after serving many employers. My friends, fellow domestic workers, were so lucky. They had higher salaries, lesser working hours and could go out every Sunday . . . I was curious why. In the library, I read about Hong Kong, about migrants . . . There, I learned about labour law for foreign domestic workers in Hong Kong.

Not many employers like their maid to be smart. They want someone smart with working, but not smart with thinking. So even if I know many things, I just hid my knowledge in front of my employer. When they said something wrong, I wouldn't talk back. When I needed to complain, I was gentle. Once when I asked my employer about my under-payment and lack of off-day, they fired me immediately. Maybe they got scared because they knew they were doing things illegally.

Even though it was they who terminated me, I had to pay the agency to find a new employer. This is why I never left any employer voluntarily even when they violated the law. It's costly to change employers and I have to consider a lot before doing so. But I did use the law to defend my rights. One Ma'am wanted to take my phone away. She said, 'I'm your employer, I will put your phone in my room. I'll give you back the phone when I come back home.' I said, 'No Ma'am, you cannot do that to me. My passport and my phone are my private property, you cannot keep them. If you keep my phone, I can report you to the police.'

99 per cent of domestic workers in Hong Kong have no private room because the apartments there are so small. Once I shared a room with a grandma and slept in a bunk bed on top of her. Even this would be considered fortunate. Many just sleep in the kitchen, or on a sofa in the living room. Some employers go to bed past midnight. If we sleep in the living room, we have to wait for them to sleep first before we can rest. It is very tiring.

Once, my employer's father harassed me. This was my worst experience. The man said, 'Yuli, do you need money? I will give you money. Just let me touch your body.' I cried and told him that I had a husband and a boy, and that it was against my religion, so he should not do that to me. I warned him that if he does anything then I would tell his son. He left angrily. But this happened again and I had to tell my employer. They asked him not to try again. But they also asked me to keep quiet and not tell others. This didn't happen again. I was lucky. There are workers whose *Ah Sir*[73] ask them for massage and blow job.

Every domestic worker lives in two worlds. There is the employer's world; where we work, learn to adapt to their culture, have to respect them and listen to them. But we also have our inner world; the place employers don't know about, our sadness, our missing our children, our anger, our fights with friends. In my early days in Hong Kong, I had a hard time learning to live in these two worlds. I had to learn how to hide emotions when I was tired or sad and act as if nothing had happened even if things were boiling inside my heart. When my

---

[73] Male employer

grandma passed away, it was a very tough time for me. She was my mother, my father, my everything. When she died, I just kept crying. Another such time was when I got divorced. I had so many questions whose answers I was looking for . . . (Laughs) Why couldn't I be like other Indonesian women who could happily stay with their family? Why—when I came overseas to build a better future—did I end up losing everything? Was I wrong to dream? Why couldn't I be a good wife? Was I not a good mother? Was I not a good woman? Why should I continue to live in this world without a meaning? Why shouldn't I kill myself by drowning in the sea, jumping from a building, or getting into an accident? Looking back, it was all very scary. I didn't even know that this was called depression. I never told my employer that I needed help. Nor did I have anyone to talk to. Nobody knew that this was happening to me. So many domestic workers experience this. When we have problems, we don't tell others. We just pray to God. This attitude is the big problem, only now I know.

Only when I started to volunteer at the Indonesian Migrant Workers Union, I realized that I was actually luckier than many. I came to know of all kinds of cases such as abuse, no pay, etc. Once, an employer went overseas, leaving the domestic worker behind with no food and no keys. Their neighbour reached out to our community for help after learning this. I wrote down instructions in Bahasa[74] on a piece of paper which the neighbour slipped into her house. She managed to run away. We then arranged a shelter for her.

Domestic workers are very stressed during the pandemic. Many of them don't get enough sleep, but have to do a lot of work like cleaning the house many times to prevent the spread of the virus. While many workers are no longer allowed to go out on off-days, they are still asked to go to the market. The employers themselves still go out freely and even organize parties with many guests at home. This is unfair. They think domestic workers spread viruses but they themselves don't.

One employer fired me after learning about my volunteer work. This Ma'am had six domestic workers before me, most of whom lasted

---

[74] Indonesian language

less than two months. She used to beat them. When she got to know about my activities, she behaved very well for some time and then fired me. I guess she was scared that I might write about her. Since then, I just told my employers that I went out taking photographs on my off-days.

I felt very angry hearing about the misery of other domestic workers. I couldn't handle these emotions so in order to let go, I wrote down their stories. To protect their identity, I never disclosed their real names. So some people suspected me of faking the stories. Of course, there are both happy and sad stories. There are many happy stories where employers and domestic workers have a good relationship. But nobody talks about our sad stories; even we migrant workers do not, for fear of making our families worried. Also, when a domestic worker does something wrong, it's all over the newspapers. But if an employer does anything wrong, no newspaper ever talks about it. It's an injustice.

Many people think that we domestic workers earn a lot of money here. They think that from what we earn here, we own big shops and big houses, cars and land in our hometown . . . Nobody understands our struggles and sufferings. Nobody asks, are you happy there? What's your experience there? Nobody cares.

My writing made my dream come true. Since I was young, I had the dream to go to Taiwan because I loved Flower Four[75]. My friends used to laugh at me for this. I actually wanted to work in Taiwan instead of Hong Kong, but the training centre said that I was too petite for Taiwan where strong bodies were in demand to take care of elderlies. But when I won the Migrant Literature Award, they invited me to Taiwan. I was so happy. There, I visited the university in Jiayi city where the drama was shot. On stage at the National Museum in Taipei, I told the audience about my love for the drama and Jerry Yan[76]. They all laughed, some told me that this museum was also a shooting location for my favourite drama! This is how my dream came true. When you have a dream, you must believe it can come true. Now, my dream is to help women domestic workers around the world.

---

[75] Boy characters in popular Taiwanese TV drama *Meteor Garden*

[76] The lead male character

My writing also got me into trouble. Once I needed to renew my visa. The immigration office was not open on Sundays. On other days, I had work. I couldn't be away, especially because I was alone at home taking care of the employer's grandmother. As a result, I was late by one week for the renewal. The immigration officers came to my employer's house and took me away in front of the grandma. They were very nice with me, and also explained to grandma that it was due to my expired visa, and that they would bring me back home after an interview. However, in the interview, they focused on my off-day activities with the worker's union. They checked my writing and photography and questioned me about my writing related to the pro-democracy protests in Hong Kong. I explained that I was not into local politics but I was writing about this to help Indonesian migrant workers understand what was happening because not many could understand the local news in English or Cantonese. With a lawyer's help, I was released, after receiving a warning from the judicial court regarding my visa renewal. I was then asked to collect my documents at a detention centre where I was told that I had to stay there and wait for my new visa. From then on, they refused to talk to me and didn't even let me speak to my lawyer. I ended up in the detention centre for twenty-eight days.

The condition in the detention centre was worse than in jail. Nobody called me by my name, only my number, as if I was not a human. I was depressed. I became so thin. They forced me to sign on a piece of paper stating that I wanted to return to Indonesia. I was not willing to sign because I didn't know if I'd be able to return to Hong Kong. But I felt threatened by them. In the end, I agreed to go back to Indonesia to wait for my visa.[77]

I was not guilty of anything. Why did they detain me? Until now I have not got an answer. Many people got detained but none told their story. That's why I need to write and let people know about what happens in the detention centre.

---

[77] https://www.abc.net.au/news/2019-12-09/hong-kong-protest-reporter-yuli-riswati-deported/11669194, accessed on 10 December 2021

Later I learned that Hong Kongers held a demonstration called 'Justice for Yuli' which is still ongoing. They held hunger strikes . . . There's a photo exhibition of the demonstration in Jakarta now. I'm waiting to complete my vaccination so that I can go to see this exhibition.

Back in Indonesia, I was hospitalized for three months. I had a cyst in my stomach because I couldn't eat anything at the detention centre. My depression continued . . . I am yet to get my visa. I have now come back to my family house. But now I look at things differently from others here. They never change—still with the same old thinking. I'm scared of being here. What if I cannot move out of this box and do what I want? My husband and I have split up. This happens to many foreign domestic workers. When we work in a new country, we enter a new world. Our mindset changes. We grow up fast. If our husbands don't grow up at the same rate, we will split up.

I think I have become more religious after working outside. I believe everything that has happened to me, whether good or bad, is by God's hand. If I could go back to my past, I would not get married so early, study harder and complete high school. I would have then grown up differently. I hope all women can be fearless about being themselves and not blindly follow other people's instructions like I did.

To the Judge, I Said 'Not Guilty'
Every Time

Rajendra (name changed), Nepal, thirty-five years old,
Activist, Store worker in Malaysia

I come from Chitwan District in Western Nepal, close to the border with India. My father was a driver. We are three brothers and two sisters. All of us are married. I have been married for ten years. I don't have children yet.

I studied in Nepal. I did a Diploma in Electrical Engineering and also studied Computer Graphic Design. I used to run a Computer Training Institute in my hometown. I was also involved in community work. I worked for twenty-seven months for a JICA[78] project on capacity development for water health. People in my community respected my work. Then the Madheshi riots happened in Nepal. All roads, shops, everything, was shut down. I had to close down my Computer Training Institute as well.

I had some Nepali friends in Malaysia who asked me to come over and work in a shop until the situation in Nepal improved. So in 2014, I came over to Malaysia. It is ironic. I used to advise my brothers

---

[78] Japan International Cooperation Agency

and friends that you should not emigrate. But I had to do this myself because of the circumstances.

Once I landed in Kuala Lumpur, I was shocked. The immigration officers made all of us workers sit on the floor in one small room. When we asked for drinking water, they said 'No'. They didn't even let us go to the toilet. They spoke to us using bad language, abusive words. I wondered how anyone could treat another human like that. Till the company came to receive the worker, the officers didn't let him out. Some had been stuck there for five days. They hadn't even eaten properly all this while. These immigration officers were forcing us to buy phone SIM cards from them. Imagine, officials peddling SIM cards. After seven or eight hours, people from my company arrived and took me out.

I was going to work in a convenience store. After two days of training they put me in a hostel near to my workplace. Then came another shock. There were so many bed bugs. I hadn't seen any bed bugs in Nepal. I just couldn't sleep. I saw some people in the hostel sleeping outside their rooms to avoid the bugs. I did the same.

One day, two months after I had started working, I was sitting a little further away from my store. It was break time. A few policemen approached me. They asked for my passport. I told them that it was with the company and I only had photocopies. They said that won't do. They took me to the police station. There had rounded up about twenty-five people there, some Indians, some Turkish. I was not worried because I thought that my company would come soon and take me out. The police took away everything we had. They even took away my glasses. I said I couldn't see without them. But they still took it away. They made me change into lock-up clothes and put me in a seven feet by seven feet room with five others. For dinner, they gave us stale rice and a small hard piece of chicken. I said I can't eat that because I was a vegetarian since childhood. They said they don't have anything else. For six days, I ate nothing. The other cellmates said, just eat. So finally I relented.

After fourteen days, they took us to a court. The judge asked, '*Salah, tak salah?*' I didn't understand. Then he said in English, 'Guilty or not guilty?' I said, 'Not guilty.' He said, 'Okay.' After that, they put me in a big jail. They gave me jail clothes and a blanket. There were more than a hundred people there in my cell. People had painted and written many things on the cell walls. There were maps of countries, flags, all sorts of things. Some were from a long time ago. It was so interesting. Some Bangladeshi and Indian inmates asked me to come and settle down next to them. They said, 'Over there is the Malay section, there is the Chinese section, so you can stay here, in our side.' I was happy to find some kinship.

I had read so much about jails, and also seen jails on TV. So I had this secret desire to be inside a jail someday, only for a few days and not for long. Strangely this happened to me in Malaysia. What can I say?

In the jail, I saw strange things.

Sometimes, there was no water to drink. We just drank from the toilet faucet. Imagine! At home, I was so choosy with food; if there was any small pebble or hair—even my own hair—in my food, I would shove the plate away. But in the jail, I ate food mixed not just with my hair but other people's hair, people I didn't even know. Why did I have to suffer all this? There was nothing out of order with my documents. I heard from others that they have a quota to fill up jails and that's why they catch migrant workers like me.

In the jail, we waited all day for our serial numbers to be announced. Maybe our country's embassy had come for us, maybe our company had sent for us. I still vividly remember my number, XXX (number changed). I had memorized it. I had waited for so long to hear that number.

There were many nice people in the jail. Some were highly educated. There was some kind of brotherhood among us South Asians inside. We shared the food that our friends or relatives from outside sent for us. I am still in touch with two of them. The imprisoned locals were different; they didn't treat us well.

Once I had a skin issue. The doctor gave me some cream wrapped in a newspaper. I said, why are you wrapping like this, the medicine will get spoilt? The doctor asked, 'Why are you saying that, what's your education?' When he heard my answer, he actually asked me to be his assistant in the jail.

There was a drug dealer from Sri Lanka in the jail. His cell was so lavish, almost like a hotel. He lived like a VIP. When I met him, I told him that I had heard of Prabhakaran, the leader of the Liberation Tigers of Tamil Eelam. He was so surprised. He said, 'You are just a kid from Nepal. How do you know about Prabhakaran?' This VIP always treated me very nicely.

After one month, they took me to the court again. The judge asked again, '*Salah, tak salah*?' I said again, 'Not guilty.' Then they took us back to the jail. This kept happening. During my third visit to the court, I asked, 'Can I say something? If you don't let me say anything, how will you understand my situation?' They asked, 'Do you have a lawyer?' I said, 'No, but this is the name of my company.' Then they said, 'Okay, we will contact the company.' After two months and fifteen days, the company came and submitted my passport and I was released.

I asked my company, 'What took you so long?' They said that usually if someone is not released within fourteen days then it takes a lot of effort, lawyer, money, etc., to get the worker released, so they thought that in any case, the police would release me in two or three months so why spend all this money after me. I then asked them to pay my salary for all this while but they said, 'No, no! No work, no pay.' I went to the Nepalese Embassy to complain but they said, 'What's the point? If you complain then they will fire you and send you back. Instead, just accept what has happened and start working again.'

I couldn't even contact my family all this while. When they finally heard from me, they asked me to come back to Nepal. I said, 'No, since I have come here with a purpose, let me do what I came to do here.'

After my release, I contacted many NGOs working with migrant workers like North-South Initiative, Tenaganita, etc. I told them about my situation. I have been working with them ever since to help other migrant workers. Right now we are working on a COVID-19 vaccination drive for migrant workers. During the early days of the pandemic, many companies were shut down. Migrant workers were locked up and they were not even paid salaries. They didn't have anything to eat. The illegal workers suffered the most. Some even committed suicide. I managed to raise 65,000 ringgit and organized emergency food supplies. We have also been arranging vitamins etc. for migrant workers. I, too, caught COVID. And I started eating chicken again after that, hoping for a faster recovery.

I have been trying to organize Nepali migrant workers here. Of course, just like in Nepal, here also they group themselves in committees along caste and tribe lines, like Brahmins have separate groups, Maoists have their own, Newaris, Christians, Congress Party followers, each have their own. But here in Malaysia, they don't fight like they do in Nepal. Together with NGOs, we try to arrange legal advice to those in need. Sometimes, some migrant workers need emergency funds and we try to arrange that. We are much better organized now, although informally. The Bangladeshis are not so well organized. I hope to get them organized too.

I just want to work in Malaysia for another year, until this COVID situation becomes better. Then I want to go back to Nepal and do something there. I want to use my knowledge with computers, my editing skills, and my photography skills. The savings in Malaysia are not enough. We make only 1,100–1,200 ringgit a month out of which 300–400 ringgit gets spent on all the expenses we have. Then if you have any health issue, often the company doesn't support it so you save even less. Then you need to work at least one year to repay the loans you took to come here. If we work as hard in Nepal as we do here, we would save more in Nepal. For those who want to come as migrant workers, I still say that being overseas is not as good as it seems. I get so many calls from Nepal asking, 'When will Malaysia allow travel again? We want to come'. I tell them if you spend ten hours working in a field in Nepal, you can save more. Or if you really must go out then it's better that you go to India, at least you can go back to Nepal easily.

I get about 300 calls a day from migrant workers asking for help. Do you know that on an average, nine migrant workers from Nepal die every week in Malaysia? People go to sleep alive, looking fine, and then they don't wake up anymore. Over 90 per cent of these deaths are 'sudden deaths', cardiac issues. But we don't know the actual reason, they just write 'heart attack'. The migrant workers are tired, they don't get leave, they have work pressure, there's pressure from family. Their wives say send money home otherwise they will divorce. And then some Nepalis drink a lot, often counterfeit alcohol, especially dangerous if drunk after vaccination. Many became blind recently after they drank heavily after vaccination. There are so many issues. Recently, a company was trying to block some workers from going back home. We helped them. That company then tried hard to get me deported, even sending some people to my room. That issue is solved now. But sometimes I do feel scared.

I tell other migrant workers that you should tell your real story to those back home. Don't just paint a rosy picture about your life as a migrant worker, tell them the real story. Don't be ashamed. If you don't tell the truth in life, there will never be any change.

An Illegal Worker, I Slept with Snakes in the Jungle

Figo Kurniawan (Indonesia), forty-seven years old,
Communications Manager, former factory worker in Malaysia

I was born in Malang, in East Java. I have two sisters and three brothers. I am number three among my siblings. My parents were civil servants. Now they are retired. I studied till SMA[79] and then started working in a factory in Sidoarjo. This was in 1992. I was eighteen years old then.

I lost my job in 2003 and was unemployed for three years. I was willing to take up any job then. I thought of going to Malaysia. I first came to Malaysia in 2006 with a legit visa and got a job in a chicken farm. Two months later I failed my medical test and so I couldn't get the work permit. The company sent me back. The same year, I came to Malaysia again, but this time with a tourist visa. I became an illegal worker, working in a factory in Selangor that manufactured steel beams. After a year, I applied for the work permit. I paid 3,500 ringgit. This time it was easier. I had friends there who helped me with each step. I passed all the tests. I became legal.

I went to Malaysia because I thought that our Indonesian culture is similar to that of Malaysia. The language is similar as well. I thought

---

[79] Equivalent to Senior High School

it would be much harder for me to adjust in other countries like Korea or Japan. Their language would have been very difficult for me to pick up. These places were much further away too. But as for Malaysia, even though the salary was lower, it would be almost like staying home.

The reality was that in Malaysia, we Indonesians faced non-stop discrimination. There was a lot of jealousy and sarcasm towards us too. The Malay people there would often tell us Indonesians, 'What, what, what? You Indonesian people? You have a very good life here yeah? Your country is in a mess but you are very happy here yeah?' They couldn't tolerate us doing well even just a little bit. Most people there think that an Indonesian migrant worker represents the lowest level of society. They say we are stupid. But I think that this attitude is not about the country or a culture, but it's the individual who brings such an attitude.

While in Malaysia, I never changed my job. Any new job would have meant learning new skills. Instead, I continued in the same company and gained more experience on the job. I had been working for ten years. It was getting better and better for me. But then, in 2016, the Malaysia government changed the rules. They said that migrant workers who have worked in Malaysia for more than ten years would no longer be able to renew their permit. But I decided to stay on. I became an illegal worker, again.

While I was an illegal worker, I never had any problem from the police. Maybe I was just lucky. Our friends at work—those who were legal—would tell us when a raid was likely. Whenever they gave the warning, I ran away from the dormitory. We would hide in the forest nearby and stay there for a few days. We came out during the day to work and then disappeared in the forest at night. The dormitory was next to the worksite and our things were locked up there. Our legally employed friends would inform us when it was safe to come back and take our things. During raids, they would tell the police that all those like us, whose lockers were locked, had gone back to their country already.

The raids always happened at night. When the warning came, everyone would be like run, run, run. Once we were too late and

I barely managed to hide behind a bus. I was so scared. When we stayed in the forest, all we had was our wallet and handphone, put in a small bag. Factory, Dormitory, Jungle; I wouldn't go anywhere else. Only once in a while, I would go to a nearby supermarket to buy things. Those are my worst memories, of having to run, hide, and sleep in the deep jungle. Life was hard, there was no bed, no shelter, no roof, and no blanket. Toilet was in the open, natural, a bit farther away from where we slept. But all that was okay. There were mosquitoes and snakes but I was not scared of them. What I was only scared of was being caught by the police. They were far more fearsome than anything else. This is how I lived for two whole years, in constant fear.

In 2019, I came back home under an amnesty program by the Malaysian government for all illegal workers. I planned to return to Malaysia after a few months, with a legal visa. But I found that my name was in a blacklist so this was no longer possible. This was also the time when COVID struck. I became unemployed again. I called many friends around Indonesia, asking for a job. Many people knew me because of my part-time work as a journalist on migrant issues in Malaysia. Whenever I had some free time, I wrote stories, poems and news articles to describe the situation and feelings of migrant workers. I wanted to show that migrant workers are not the scum of the earth. I wanted to show that we are not stupid. In fact, in 2017, I was given an award by the Indonesian Ministry of Foreign Affairs for my journalism. Because of all this, I was eventually hired by the Indonesian Migrant Worker Union as their Head of Media and Communications. Now I am based in Jakarta.

Yes, I faced so many challenges in Malaysia but I still want to go back and work there. The reason is purely economic. Maybe my friend can get me a job there again.

I feel proud because I was a migrant worker. Our government says that we migrant workers are the *pahlawan*[80] of the nation. But that's not why I feel proud. I feel proud because as a migrant worker, I am the hero for my own family. I am the hero for their future. Because of what

---

[80] Heroes

I experienced, I know now that I can do everything and anything for my family. For their sake, I can face any danger. I went through all this so that my children don't have to live my life.

I Hated My Village, I Love It Now

R Vijayakanth (India), thirty years old, Project Engineer in Singapore

I was born in a village called Udaikulam in Tamil Nadu. The name Udaikulam comes from the many pools in the village. I have two older sisters. I hold a Diploma in Mechanical Engineering. I have been a migrant worker in Singapore since 2013, starting as a technician in a racking company and then as project engineers in crane companies.

My father and mother are nomadic pastoralists. They keep sheep and goats. All year round, they roam from village to village visiting the fields of farmers. The farmers pay for the fertilizer they get from the droppings of the animals. They stay for a few months in one place and then move to another. This is an ancient lifestyle. We have been doing this for generations. We also sell the young males who are then trained to fight, for betting sports. Some are sold for meat. My parents also have a small farm where they grow onions, chillies, etc.

My childhood was so fun. As my itinerant parents were always away, I was at home mostly with my two sisters and my blind grandmother. My sisters, only a few years older than me, didn't ask me any questions. There was no one to scold me. I didn't need to be scared of anyone. We played cricket all day. I would swim in the pools for four or five hours daily. Sometimes I played for so long that I didn't even bother to eat. Because of this carefreeness, I almost had a fatal accident. I was only eight years old then. My eldest sister gave me some money to buy snacks from a nearby village. I was so happy to have the money; I was running fast, my eyes closed. A big truck was speeding by, carrying several gas cylinders. Just when I was about to be hit, the truck came to a halt. Luckily, the gas cylinders inside the truck were empty. If they were full, that would have been full stop for me because the truck couldn't have braked in time.

My eldest sister was like my mother. She cooked for us every day. When she got married—you know in Indian culture—we had to give money, gold and gifts as dowry. Whether you have money or not, if you are the girl's family, you have to pay dowry. My father had to give twenty-five ounces of gold. Because we were a lower middle-class family, we became quite poor after her wedding. Around the same time, my grandmother died. So just my second sister and I were left in the house. Life became very hard. There was no one to take care of us. Our parents sent us some money through relatives but we just didn't know how to cook. Some nights, we just slept without eating anything.

In my first job in Singapore, I worked only with Chinese people. The bosses were Singaporeans but my fellow workers and supervisors were all from China, all six of them. They didn't speak any English, not even simple English. But I still needed to work with them. I couldn't understand anything they said. When they looked at me, I guessed that I had to do something. It was very hard. Not just that. The company made me stay in the same room with them. So I was stuck with them for twenty-four hours a day for three long years. They were also stuck with me. Very funny. The first day at work, they took me to a Chinese stall for lunch. I had never eaten Chinese food before. Within the first few bites, I vomited, right in front of them. Imagine! Now it all seems funny. Not so back then.

The Chinese supervisor used to scold me a lot. He was really terrible. Maybe they were jealous, because I had S Pass while the Chinese workers had only Work Permits[81]. I tried not to get bothered.

---

[81] Migrant workers on S Pass typically have higher salaries than those on Work Permit

My friends told me many times, 'If you come to work in Singapore, don't complain about anything, if they scold you, keep your feelings to yourself.' One day, this Chinese supervisor scolded me using bad words. He must have been using bad words all along but that day, from the little Chinese I had already picked up, I knew the meaning. I became very angry. I went and complained to the big boss. The boss said, 'It is okay, we cannot control the China people, you just try to become friends with them.'

Slowly, I started picking up some Chinese. Every day I learnt one new word. I showed them things and asked them what it was called. They also needed my help from time to time. So after three months, they became friendlier. They started trying the food I cooked. I also tried their food, without vomiting. Sometimes, we played together. We began making fun of each other. They were also nice people.

We were all very scared in the early days of COVID. So many migrant workers were getting infected. We saw videos from Italy and China, people catching COVID and suddenly falling dead on the streets. So many rumours were going around. When I saw such videos, I wondered whether I could ever go back home or would I just end up dead here in Singapore. My family was even more scared hearing the news from Singapore. But I just kept telling them the good things.

Something strange happened during that period. There was a worker from my company who had not gone out of his dormitory since he had come to Singapore. His wedding got arranged and then got postponed. Finally, after a long time, the company gave him leave and the ticket to go back. I was asked to send him off to the airport. The worker had caught COVID earlier. So he thought that everything he had, still had the virus. Before going to the airport, he threw away all his clothes, his luggage and everything he had because he was worried about carrying the virus home. He threw everything into the rubbish bin. Looking at him, I began feeling so anxious about my own situation. Before leaving, the man wanted to buy some gifts for his family. We dropped by at Tekka Market. The man wanted to buy some toys for his nephew. When we went inside the toy shop, something strange happened to me. Maybe because I was feeling anxious. I began playing with the toys on display. First, I took the toy gun and shot randomly.

Then I took the tiger, then Superman, the monkey, the car; for fifteen or twenty minutes or I don't know how long, I played with each and every toy. I forgot about everything else. I felt like a child again. When we finally came out of the toy shop, I had become a new person. My mind was so fresh, so clear. I was seeing a new world. It was a very grateful feeling. The other worker bought a helicopter.

I got married in 2018. It was an arranged marriage. That is the culture in my hometown. At first, my family would ask for the girls' horoscopes and check if they matched with mine, whether we were made for each other, that is the culture there. Only when the horoscopes matched, my sister and brother-in-law went to see those girls. They found one in a village about thirty kilometres from ours. Then the girl and I talked over the phone, whether we like each other, whether our lifestyle, everything okay. I really liked her because she is very pretty and kind-hearted. She also has a Master's Degree and was working as a Physical Education teacher. Everything was good.

When I got married, we didn't ask for any dowry. I fought with my father and mother saying we shouldn't ask for any. Of course, her family still gave some gifts because they think that given their social standing, they ought to give something. But till today, I haven't asked my wife what she really got.

We had been together for only seventeen days in the first two years of our married life. I wanted to be with her so much. But there was no way. Only last year, we were finally together for much longer, because of COVID. I had taken two month's leave but because of restrictions I couldn't come back to Singapore. So I ended up spending seven months back home. Actually, this was also the longest time I have been with my parents, because they were nomadic pastoralists when I was young. So this time, when I was leaving, my parents were all crying for the first time. This was so precious for me.

My wife is seven months pregnant. Once my child is born, I hope to go back home for at least one week. But now with Omicron, every day this COVID is just increasing and increasing. My bosses are willing to let me go but I don't know what will happen. I feel guilty and nervous about this. Especially because the last time, I got trapped in India for seven months when my leave was only for two months. I feel guilty towards my wife. But I am also anxious about my job.

I don't want to remain a migrant worker forever. Maximum, three more years. 2025—I want to go back home. My parents are getting old. I want to be with my wife as well. During my last stay at home, I helped with my parent's sheep and goats. I worked in the farmland. I started liking that lifestyle too. Now I want to preserve my family's ancestral profession.

There are migrant workers in Singapore who have been here for twenty-five years or more. They miss their family so much. Like, I have a cousin who came here twenty-seven years ago. I remember him coming to our home when I was only four years old. He had given me chocolates back then. He is still in Singapore. He is fifty years old now. He counts the number of days he has been with his family, less than 700. He tells me, 'Don't stay here, go back fast. If you want to make money, make it fast. You see my example—I lost everything, everything that matters. I wasted my life already, everything is now gone.'

Earlier, I didn't like my village, But ever since I came to Singapore, I began appreciating my village more. Now I want to protect nature in my village. Earlier, I have had no such thoughts, not just when I was a child, but even when I was in my twenties.

Now, whenever I go back to India, I bring the local schoolchildren to plant trees in my village. As a reward, I buy a lot of gifts for them, like books, geometry boxes; necessary things for kids. When I give them these gifts, I ask them to not just plant trees but also to take care of them. All this change of thinking has happened since I came to Singapore. I look at the history of Singapore and how it has worked hard to keep itself green. I always tell my friends, 'We cannot change our whole country, we cannot even change our state, but we can at least change our village.' When I say this, most don't listen to me. But I don't care about that. I can get moving first. I believe that change cannot happen suddenly but can happen gradually. The first time I planted a tree, I was so shy. I was so conscious that people were watching me. They were also talking behind my back unnecessarily, like, 'Is he going to change our village or what? What does he think, just because he lives abroad?' But as I keep planting more trees, they have started asking me in a nicer way, 'Why do you keep planting trees?' Slowly, they are starting to support me. I mean, throw the seeds today and then the fruits will come tomorrow, that's what I believe. There are now fifty new trees from this. Seven of those trees have become big.

Regarding preserving my family's ancestral profession, nomadic pastoralism is a dying trade. Twenty years back, there were no chemical fertilizers so there was demand for the services of my parent's sheep and goats. But now, chemical fertilizers are so cheap. It's everywhere. No one cares for our goats and sheep anymore. Other such nomads from my parent's generation have already sold off their animals. Their children have studied and are not doing this anymore. But I want to continue this in some way. My parents are in their seventies, but they still keep running around because they have always been nomads. So last year, I bought ten acres of land in my village so that my father and mother could take care of it and finally settle down. But I still want to keep all our goats and sheep. We know each one of them. We know the colour variations of each. We know what each one's temperament is like. We never eat them. Of course, sometimes we sell them to others who may kill them and sell their meat. So if we eat meat, we go to some faraway market to buy, we don't buy from our village market where our goats and sheep may accidentally end up. When I come back for good, I want to take care of our animals. I feel sentimental about them. I feel sentimental about our heritage.

The Internet Changed Me, But Singapore Gave Me the Chance to be Free

A.K. Zilani (Bangladesh), twenty-nine years old,
Maintenance Worker in Singapore

I come from a village in Cumilla district. We are three brothers. My father ran small businesses. Sometimes he traded jute, sometimes, other things. He never made a lot of money. I was born rather late in my father's life. In my earliest memories of him, he already had white hair.

In school, I was always the first boy in class. All the way from class one to five, I stood first. Even after that I was always either the third or fourth student. But my downfall began from class nine. I got transferred to a new school. It was a famous school. It was in a bigger village and had many more students. I had difficulty adjusting. I have always been an introvert. So it was hard for me to make new friends there. Also, the teachers there were all so difficult. There was this one maths teacher in particular who used to tease me a lot. I was always a little weak in maths, so this teacher took to insulting me. He would beat me as well. He would call me to the blackboard and insult me in front of everyone saying, 'This boy comes from a school in ruins so his studies are also in ruins.' And if anything bad happened in the school, he would always blame me for that. So I started skipping classes. Some days I would just attend school for half the day and go out just before the maths class. I would just walk around aimlessly to kill time.

I remember one day vividly. That day this maths teacher had come across my father in the market. He complained a lot about me. When father came home he was very sad. He said, 'My eldest son is useless and the other child is also no good in studies. You were my only hope and I had to hear all this about you.' He beat me badly. He said that he would commit suicide and left home all of a sudden. We all believed him. A train line passed through just behind our house. So many people have died there, some by suicide. My mother was wailing. She was blaming me. I was sitting motionless in one corner. I was just stunned. Eventually, my father came back.

So that's how my downfall began. At school, I was worried about getting beaten. At home, I was worried about getting beaten. So my results were not good from then on.

Just after my college exams, I had a break for a few months. I enjoyed that time a lot. I used to go around stealing fruits from our neighbour's gardens. Once I tried to steal a jackfruit but I fell down from the tree and broke my hand. There was another incident with the *Taal*[82] fruit. There was a Taal fruit farm in our village. The owner was so strict and stingy that he didn't even let his own children touch his fruits. So one day we friends planned to steal his fruits. It happened just so that some elders had also made the same plan. My friends were already up on the trees when the other group came. They began chasing us because we had the fruits already. Eventually they caught some of us. But we all sat together and shared the fruits and had such a great laugh. The owner's own son was part of that other group.

My elder brother went to work in Saudi Arabia but returned after three years. At that time, our family was having financial difficulties. My father borrowed money and then sent him to Dubai. But again, he returned after one year—he is a completely failed project.

---

[82] Asian Palmyra Palm

Around then, I had just done my schooling and was applying to universities. Eventually, I got an admission for an honours degree in economics. But to study in any university, I would have to stay in the city, away from home. I would need money for my accommodation, food and transport. Moreover, it would take another few years before I could get a job. With an unemployed elder brother, and another brother who was still studying, my father just didn't have any way to support my education.

One of my friends, who was working in Singapore, told me to come over to Singapore. I borrowed more than 10,000 Singapore dollars to fund my move to Singapore. This was back in 2010. It took me almost two years to repay all the loans.

When I first came to Singapore, I had to transit via Malaysia. In Malaysia, the officials treated us like animals. They made us all sit on the floor and didn't let us eat or drink or even go to the toilet. One even said, 'You pee when you reach Singapore.'

I reached Singapore the next day, early in the morning. I was extremely hungry. I had only eight or ten dollars in my pocket. The first thing I did upon landing was to head to a twenty-four-hour restaurant called Sri Maju in Little India. There I had *thosai* for the first time in my life and some coconut chutney. It tasted so nice. I can still feel it in my tongue. I still get lost in random thoughts when I walk past Sri Maju.

I, like most migrant workers, had no real clue about what work I will eventually get in Singapore. My training in Bangladesh was on electrical stuff. But the employer ignored all that. I don't even know what my salary will be. For my first day at work, they took me to the site in a lorry. Along the way, I saw so many big buildings. There was nothing like this back home. I was mesmerized. The lorry stopped at a construction site. Only at that moment did I realize that this was my fate. My tummy began churning.

My employer was a manpower supplier company. Such companies pay very little. I got paid only eighteen dollars a day. Such supplier companies make you work very hard to squeeze every bit out of you. They gave me the task of mixing cement and carrying bricks. I had never done such work in my life. Actually, I had never done any hard labour before. Back home, I just used to help my father a little with his field every now and then. So I was overwhelmed when they handed me the spade. But what could I do? The boss scolded me always. Once he made me run carrying two heavy cement buckets. That was my punishment for being slow. I stepped on a nail, it went through my feet. I was in terrible pain. But I couldn't stop. Within two days, I got enormous blisters on my hand. The next two days, I couldn't even work because of that. My boss used such vulgar words to scold me. I cried when I was alone. That was my worst day in Singapore.

Within the first week, some new workers asked for a change of work. Like me, they too couldn't take the hard labour. But I was scared that if I asked for a change then I would be sent back like my brother. I was too afraid. I have always been a bit of a fearful person since childhood, you see. I didn't want to be like my elder brother. I had to support the family. I just bit my tongue and bore all the pain.

I was put up in a shelter at the worksite itself. Ten of us shared a room. I had no privacy or personal life. I had to wake up at 8 a.m. and go to work immediately, and then come back at ten in the night, then cook and sleep by twelve. Even on Sundays, I used to work till ten in the night. In one whole year, I stepped out of the site only twice, to buy phone cards. This is not called life. This is slavery.

I didn't have many friends in Singapore, just a few whom I had met at the training centre at Dhaka. At the shelter, there was another guy from my district. He used to protect me and help me, especially with cooking. I didn't know anything about cooking then. So he was the one who cooked most of the days. Some days when he came too late from work, he would just ask me to prepare whatever I could. Once I cooked chicken with yam. Everyone was laughing. I said why are you all laughing? This is a brand new recipe. Try it.

But not everyone was nice. At another site, I was put up with very tough people. I remember this person from Bangladesh called Bulbul. I shared the cooking with him and three others. This Bulbul always complained about me; 'This boy doesn't cut the vegetables properly, this, that,' non-stop, like a mother-in-law. He even complained about me at work, to my supervisor. Once I had an argument with him after which we stopped talking. I decided to manage my own meals. But for a few days, I just ate bread and bananas. This Bulbul used to tease me about my low pay. He boasted that he was earning thirty-five dollars a day. I told him that you are making this much after working in Singapore for twelve years; I will be earning more than you in just two years, and then I will show you my pay-slip. Indeed when I joined a new company after one year, I began making thirty-five dollars a day. I have been looking for Bulbul to show my pay slip.

I didn't tell my family what my work was or how my life was. I didn't have the courage. I just said that all was well. But my mother guessed my reality. She used to weep that I worked so hard only to send all my savings back. But I asked her what was wrong with that? Didn't father work hard all his life to pay for our upbringing? So what was wrong with what I was doing?

Once a manager from one of the companies where I was placed by the supplier company saw me running around, working non-stop. He asked me if I would like to join him directly instead. I took up his offer and have been with them since then. Here, I work in maintenance. The pay is better. Well, it is not very high. All I can say is that I think I'm now doing better than many other migrant workers in Singapore. But there are also many migrant workers who are doing better than me. Well, at least I have a lot more freedom now. I've made many friends and connections in this company. You can say that I have found my own place here. That's how I console myself.

I enrolled myself in a driving school because the pay is much higher for drivers. But because of COVID, the school was closed just after three classes. I would also like to get trained so I can join a facility-maintenance company. That's what I hope.

For the last few years, I have been part of a few organizations like the theatre. Together with a few friends, I also organized cultural shows by migrant workers and started a library for migrants. I love the theatre a lot. I don't really have a creative side but this theatre work helps me feel more confident. Now I am less scared of talking to people. I can speak English better. The theatre work has also helped me physically because of all the body movements involved.

My favourite activity here is to spend time with my freethinker friends. Since 2014, I have been a freethinker. You can trace this to my childhood. Introverted people like me have their own world. So as a kid, more than talking, I liked listening, and reading. I read a lot of newspapers and magazines. When the US attacked Afghanistan, every house in Bangladesh had Bin Laden's picture framed. Even my house had one. But through my reading of magazines and newspapers, I knew he was not a hero. Then why worship him? I used to think differently from others. My mind went everywhere; like if Allah created the universe then who created Allah? I found the story of Adam and Eve and Satan just a fantasy. I wondered why are there still other religions in this world if Islam is arguably the best and the strongest. To have such thoughts you don't need to be a philosopher, you just need some common sense. But still I did all the religious stuff. I would pray. I fasted during the holy month of Islam. Many people are self-contradictory like me; they have doubts but then think of an after-life or are scared of society and therefore still continue their religious duties.

Around 2014–2015, the well-known freethinker Abhijit Roy and many other freethinkers were hacked to death in Bangladesh, I got the news in my Facebook feeds. At that time I didn't even know what freethinker meant. But after hearing about their tragic deaths, I began reading their blogs. There I found answers for many of my doubts. There I also found many more people like me. That's how I became a freethinker.

The Bangladeshi new generation has two types of people. One of these two is the hypocrite, they want to stay religious while enjoying all benefits of modern life. They don't see the contradiction. Then the other type is the extremist, their brains are full of nothing but cow dung. They study in the madrassah. Their awareness of the world is limited to what Mullahs say on stage. In my previous dormitory, there were many extremists. I don't have a problem working or interacting with religious people. My problem is with religion not with the person. And I have the right to have an opinion about religion because it is affecting the state of the society I live in. But they don't understand such points. You must have heard about the Hindu idols and temples that were burnt recently in Bangladesh. They posted on Facebook that some Hindus put a Koran on Hanuman's feet and that started the violence. Is this possible? Do Hindus in Bangladesh have so much courage to put a Koran in Hanuman's feet? The Hindus in Bangladesh are meek like wet cats; they live in total fear there. I have seen my own Hindu neighbours. I have grown up with Hindus. I know their condition. They live in ghettos. Anyway, I have become more careful. I don't talk much about freethinking. Who knows who will get hurt when and how and do something stupid? My friends on Facebook and in my theatre group do know that I am a freethinker. Actually, I have removed many religious people from my Facebook friends list. People back home don't know. If my family knows, they will bring the whole house down (laughs).

I have always worked hard to help my family. I gave money to my younger brother to come to Singapore for a few years as a migrant worker. I have especially done a lot for my elder brother. I set up two shops for him. He wasted both. I paid for a fishpond and a cow farm so he can run those. In total I have spent over 14–15 lacs taka on him. That's a big amount in Bangladesh. But he has not been successful in anything. He only bought bulls to sell during *Korban*. Bulls mean huge running costs but no running income. That's why I had told him to buy some cows too so they can give milk and generate running income. But he won't listen to me. The only thing I don't yet do for him is to give him pocket money. And my useless brother still complains. The man has three kids and I have been supporting them for ten years. What kind of a person is that? There is no peace in the house because of this.

Earlier I used to send back all my savings every month. I have stopped doing that now. I only send money home when there is some emergency. I want to take care of myself too. I bought a second hand cycle in Singapore. I do long distance cycling now. Since COVID began, I have become more careful with my health. I am twenty-nine now and I want to stay healthy even when I am old. And since I don't want to have kids, there won't be anyone to take care of me later. That's why I stopped having sweet drinks, stopped eating fried food, and even bought some bands to do exercise in my room.

My family wants to get me married. But I have been giving one excuse after another. The recent excuse is that I need to build a house first before starting a family. Now the house will be built in two months. So my parents will be pressurizing again. But I don't want to get married. If I get married in Bangladesh, I will have self-contradiction with my beliefs. Because I am a migrant worker, my wife will have to stay in Bangladesh with my parents, do housework, and follow the culture that is prevalent there. I can't agree with that. I don't like the thought of seeing my dearest person live a life like that. And if we have children, he or she will have to grow up in that same social context and then become like them. I don't want that to happen. If at all I find someone who thinks like me, I don't even want to have my own kids. I would rather adopt.

I want to stay in Singapore as long as possible. That is because I want to avoid Bangladesh as long as possible. In all these years, I have gone back only three times. Each time, I couldn't bear to stay for longer than a month. My mentality has become totally different from the friends I grew up with. I find it hard to get along. Everyone has become so religious. I have arguments with them whenever I talk about religion, politics or society. Like some aspects of our culture are just superstitions, but they will argue when I say so. So whenever I go back, I just stay inside our house. There I spend time sweeping the floor or watering the garden, the small housework I used to do as a child.

I don't think Singapore is responsible for changing my outlook. I think it is the internet that changed me. But Singapore gave me the chance to be free. When I am in Bangladesh, I still have to keep up the pretenses. Even now when I go back home and when it's time to read the *namaaz*, mother asks, 'Why are you not going to the mosque, it's just next to the house?' So I go to the mosque and pretend. Here, in this foreign city, I am free from all that baggage.

Part VII

In this section, migrant workers dwell on topics ranging from love, romance, racism, religion, homesickness, among others.

Potpourri of Musings

Love in a Foreign Land

Wiwi, Deni, Sugi; all migrant workers from Indonesia to Singapore, working as domestic workers

Deni: Some men hunt us girls for money. Women from broken families are easy targets: they fall in love easily, give out cash when their boyfriend asks . . . They only know the guy from Facebook, know nothing about their real identity, job, where they stay, permit/ID number, etc. But the girl still gives everything, goes to the hotel and sleeps with the guy. She gets pregnant and then the guy is nowhere to be found.

Some guys are from those countries where they have arranged marriages. They have chosen wives at home, but they also have ladies here to play and have fun; they call it 'dating'. Such temporary couples are happy with each other, but when it's time to go home, they will go to their arranged wives.

Wiwi: Here cheating is normal. Many guys keep sending Facebook messages to girls. Very easy, no? Stressed girls are easy targets on Facebook. Many girls are very stressed working in their employers' houses. They want to have fun when going out. The men can give her the fun, or 'one-night-stand love'.

Girls also get stressed because of how the boys behave. Initially they flirt every day texting you a lot, 'Hi good morning baby, are you having your breakfast? Had your lunch? Baby, what are you doing now?' After they get you once, they are gone.

Deni: Some girls date expatriates[83], hoping the man will marry her and give her a brighter future.

Sugi: There's also peer pressure. When your friends have boyfriends, you feel you need one too. If your friend has an expatriate boyfriend, you feel like getting one 'white man'. (laugh)

Deni: Dating in Singapore is just playing. You cannot use your heart: 'I love this man'. No, it's just 'we are going out'. But if I don't feel emotionally attached, I cannot just go around with someone to pass time. But if I feel emotionally attached, I'll start to care and have expectations to stay together. Then it becomes hard to date just for fun. Thinking about these, I get scared and want to protect myself.

Wiwi: Yeah, the first thing that I learned was to not have any expectations. I want to pass time because I have freedom. My daughter has already grown up, and I don't plan to marry again. I look for the same energy and chemistry in the man. I dated my boyfriend for three months, taking a long time to understand each other slowly. Our attitude was like, 'I don't expect anything from you so you shouldn't expect anything from me'. Some girls cry a lot or even kill themselves when the boyfriend has another girlfriend. I'd happily let the man go if he finds another girlfriend. I can find another one. Please don't disturb me.

Durga Balan (India), thirty-five years, Safety Officer in Singapore:

I had an arranged marriage. When I got married, I was already working in Singapore. But I resigned soon and spent a year with my wife back in India. I came back only after our first child was born. Overall, in the last ten years, I haven't been able to spend much time with my wife.

I speak to her every day, at least for half an hour. Whenever I have some time, I call her. I just ask whether she has taken her breakfast or lunch. So I share my feelings this way. But most of the time, we argue when on call. That is also a kind of love. Really, really.

---

[83] Refers to Caucasians in this context

Every day I feel a little guilty that my wife has to manage all by herself. Every day. I just disconnect the call with her whenever that feeling comes. And whenever she asks me about my travel plans or about moving back to India for good, I say I have another call coming. It is a really different feeling. I don't know. Really, really. Basically, she understands me, she knows my character. So she expects nothing much romantic from me.

* * *

Going Home

Md Sharif (Bangladesh), forty-two years old, Safety Coordinator in Singapore:

The day my leave gets approved, that moment I get my air ticket from my boss; that whole month from then till I am finally back home is so joyful. It feels like half of me is already home. The things we talk about when I call home become different. We are talking about what gifts to buy, we are planning things to do together; we are all happy. Then comes the joy of preparing and editing again and again the list of what gifts to buy for which relative and friend, then going around shops and markets to look around, buy, and get a bigger luggage to fit in all these. No festival compares to this personal festival of mine.

The last two weeks pass so slowly. The clock seems broken.

Once back, I am meeting so many people during those one or two months. I am telling them all about what the culture of Singapore is like. I am taking my family for a vacation to some nice place. Soon, one month is gone. Even sooner, two months are gone.

The last week is the most painful. The conversations I have with people become different; there is a tinge of sadness. I hear silences in between. I see tears appear around me. I develop a sudden attachment for my room, my village, my country. I think a few times about asking my boss for an extension. Together with family, we plan for the possibility of coming back for good. But nothing like this happens. I have to earn money to build my family's future.

The scenes at the airport are the most painful, not just mine but of all the other workers boarding the flight. I see young children clinging to their father's chest, refusing to let go, crying, having to be snatched away. These scenes make me feel sadder. Once back, it is the same dormitory, the same worksite.

Some workers adjust the moment they look away from their loved ones; these are the more experienced workers who have been away for long. But the first timers find it the hardest. They have a whole village that has come to see them off at the airport. But as time passes, the bonds with others weaken. Only the family matters. And once you have kids, they take over all the love you have. In fact, as my son grows older, my yearning to be with him only grows stronger.

Durga Balan:

Before the pandemic, I used to fly back to India every three months. Every time I went back I would take my kids to a temple or some nice place for an outing so that they are happy. But I have not seen my family in person for two years now. We have daily video calls. During those calls, I try to teach my kids a bit. They listen to me even when I am on video. They try to follow. So it is not very difficult to manage them. But of course it is different when you are together with them.

Wiwi, Sugi and Deni

Wiwi: Homesickness is very painful. Whenever I went home, I had to deal with homesickness starting from zero again.

I don't want to go back home too often for monetary reasons as well. There are many new babies (in my neighbourhood). When I see the babies, I have to give them money. I'm an elder. (laugh) The relatives always expect me to have a lot of money. They don't realize that I have to pay for many things in my own life.

I never bought gifts for them in Singapore, but in the markets back home: cheaper and easier to carry. The same chocolate sold at ten dollars for three in Singapore is ten dollars for twenty in Indonesia.

Deni: Once you start giving money to relatives, you need to do it every time you come home. I'm happy to give gifts and I always bring goodies. My mom would cook something for the neighbours to thank God for her daughter's safety. It feels great, too, because we have enough to give. But this gifting is only possible once in a while, not daily.

Sugi: You can choose not to give, be gifts or money. They ask you for presents sarcastically when you don't give them. A few years ago, I was happy to give gifts back home. But the amount I gave failed my relatives' expectations. 'Why so little? You came from Singapore and give me this little money?' When I gave chocolates, I heard comments like, 'We also have chocolate in Indonesia. Why did you buy chocolate from Singapore?' Since then, I felt discouraged and never gave up again.

How locals and others treat us

Wiwi: The neighbourhood I stay in is not very upscale. They still use the kind of insulting words like *KangNang*[84]. Sugi may not see much of this because she lives in an upscale neighbourhood.

Sugi: Well, it's not necessarily better. One day, when I went to throw trash in the public area, my American neighbour blamed me for bringing cockroaches to their house.

Deni: Somehow people can identify me as a helper. In my condo swimming pool, an auntie said to me, 'You helpers cannot swim here. If you don't leave, I will call the security guard.' I told her, 'You can call whoever you like. My employer allows me to swim here.'

Whenever I queue at Kopitiam[85] behind white people or locals, I hear the sales assistants talking very friendly with them. And when it's my turn, they speak to me in a different voice. 'Wh-at you wa-n-t!' (laugh)

Now, I'm braver. I'll protest, 'Can you please be nicer?' I don't want people to treat me any worse than others.

Sugi: The longer we stay here, the better we blend in with the locals. Sometimes this makes a difference. Even if they can tell that we are helpers, they know we can speak up and don't dare to bully us.

A.K. Zilani (Bangladesh), twenty-nine years old, Maintenance Worker in Singapore:

When I first came to Singapore, I didn't feel free. It seemed like a strange foreign place. I had zero interaction with the locals. So I kept to my comfort zone and just mingled with other Bangladeshis. But

---

[84] Domestic Workers
[85] A drinks stall in a food court or hawker centre

for the last few years, I have had some interaction with the locals, because of my theatre and other work. What I find most amusing about locals in Singapore is their opinion about migrant workers. Everyone thinks that he is an expert without knowing anything about our lives. I like reading their comments on articles about migrant workers. Like one says, 'these migrants come to our country, earn a lot and back in Bangladesh they live in big houses and have big cars, so they shouldn't get any privilege'. Isn't that completely false? Then there is this recent issue about the safety of migrant workers when they are transported in open trucks. In response, the locals will post pictures of crowded buses and trains in India and Bangladesh, people sitting on top or hanging from all sides. So they will say that we migrant workers are used to unsafe transport. But in our country, we also pee by the roadside. Will you allow me to do that in your country as well?

Durga Balan:

At my workplace, there are Tamil people, Malay people, Cantonese people. They come from Singapore, India, China, Bangladesh or Malaysia. But we are all good friends. Also for the last ten years, for most of the workers I know here, only our company names have changed. We still work for the same master contractors at the same workplace. So only our uniforms have changed but we still work together every day. We wish each other during festivals like Hari Raya or Chinese New Year. We wish birthdays, give gifts. We meet outside of work, in food courts. Moreover because I am a safety officer, they give me a lot of respect. I think only the language is different, but we workers are all the same.

But with the locals, it is different. There is a lot of racism, especially during this pandemic. Normally we hardly interact with locals but we face this when we are taking the MRT[86] or a lift in public areas. When we workers enter into the lift, the locals will not enter. Or when we workers are rushing to enter the lift, they will close the door from

---

[86] Subway train in Singapore

inside. Once I took the train from Boon Lay. It was fully empty; only one elderly person was sitting—I don't even want to mention the gender or race. When I tried to take a seat in the same row, the person just put a leg there. In the next station, some locals boarded the train and the person immediately took away the leg. Then I understood what was happening. But I try not to mind such things. These are all elderly people who do this. So I don't take these things seriously.

Do I have any good memories of locals treating us kindly? Let me think, okay, [long pause] . . . okay maybe once only. My friend and I had gone to the Botanical Garden. It was a very hot day and we had forgotten to bring along drinking water. So we were very thirsty. I don't know how some people understood what we were saying and suddenly offered us a bottle of water. We were so shocked.

* * *

Those Missed

Elpidia Abel Malicsi (The Philippines), sixty-four years old, Domestic Worker, worked in Saudi Arabia, currently working in Hong Kong:

I cried really hard when I lost my mother. I had sacrificed for her. I gave her everything I could. Though I had lost her, I also felt happy that I could give her a good life. I talked to her about all my problems. Now that she is gone, I still tell her all my problems. I just go into the bathroom and then talk to her.

Wiwi:

When I left my daughter for Singapore, she was very young. It was so hurtful to leave my baby girl behind. I couldn't stop crying whenever a baby was in my sight. Since then, I have always avoided jobs taking care of babies. I can only take care of dogs. I still cannot play with babies, even if I'd love to get close to them. Of course, I'm better now—my daughter is already nineteen! Where has all the time gone? When I left her, she was two. When I returned home, she was already six, then eleven, fifteen, and now she's nineteen!

Durga Balan:

When I was younger, my father gave me full freedom to do whatever I wanted to do. The only thing he told me was, 'If you take some decision on your own, then don't come and complain to me if something goes wrong. You have to face the consequences yourself.' I want to give the same freedom to my children. If they want my support, okay, I'm ready to support. If they don't want my support, okay, I will allow them to go their own way. Because things change with time. 2021 is nothing like how it was during my childhood. The people, kids, culture and everything has totally changed. And I don't know how things will be in another twenty years. We cannot control this change. So, we also cannot control the next generation. So if I don't have this kind of open-mindedness and instead try to control my children, I will suffer if things don't turn out right for them after twenty years. It will really hurt me also if they don't obey my words. So it is better that I give them permission to make their own decisions. The only thing I can do is to support them in whatever they want to do in a good way. I just want them to have good habits and give respect to others. That is enough. Really, really.

* * *

First Impressions

Wiwi, Sugi and Deni

Wiwi: My first impression of Singapore was, 'Wow, it's so clean.' Even the ferry I took from Batam to Singapore was so clean. I found Singapore so different from Jakarta which is hot and dirty with homeless people under the bridges; The small boats in the Singapore River were beautiful.

Everything was 'wow' till we went to the agency's office. After that? As soon as we arrived, the agency sent us for a test. We had no food for a long time. Later, we were taken to the agency's shelter, a terrace house. There were around twenty girls. The agency asked us to take turns to shower in a small toilet; we only had a small red pale of water to use. At night, we slept next to one another like fish in the market. There were just too many of us. It was seventeen years ago. That experience was also 'wow' (laugh).

Deni: I came to Singapore eight years ago. The agency said everyone in Singapore walks very fast, so I walked very fast, even at immigration. So, I got stopped at the immigration. Luckily, nothing happened. A van picked me up along with eight ladies, a mix of Burmese and Filipinos. They packed us in a small HDB with many other girls and made us sleep on roll mattresses. Oh my God! There were so many bed mites. People kept slapping them on the wall, splashing blood everywhere, leaving stains on the wall. I didn't know that bed mites drank blood!

The first day when I arrived at my employer's house, they checked my bag. I didn't feel bad because the agency had warned me of this earlier. My employer was an Indonesian-Singaporean couple. My Indonesian Ma'am was worried that I might bring black magic to make her Singaporean husband fall for me.

The agency had also told me to not take along any money, not to keep long hair, and not to wear shorts. So, I went to my employer's house penniless, with short hair and no shorts. When my employer asked me to cut my hair a year later, I said, 'Please, no, I will tie my hair so that it doesn't affect my work.' Then they asked me to cut my hair again a year later. I again said, please don't. Then my Sir, a nice Singaporean man, gave it a thought. There was a discussion about my hair in the family. In the end, the grandma in the family said, 'Okay, just make sure that no hair falls in the house.' I'm okay with this if these are the rules of the house, what can you do?

The agent also asked me not to bring a Quran, saying that Chinese people would think it's black magic. I still brought along the Quran with me. My employer took it away and returned my Quran only a year later.

Wiwi: My employer took away my Doa Guam[87] and the Quran. During those months, I felt empty. Today we can read anything on mobile phone, but I didn't have one back then. After five years of working for them, I was finally allowed to buy the Quran and all my prayer stuff.

---

[87] Muslim woman's wear for prayer

Deni: On the other hand, our people back home always think we are becoming less religious because of Singapore.

* * *

Festivals, Here and There

Md Sharif:

For all the festivals we have in Bangladesh; Eid, Victory Day, Language Day, there is a certain life, joy and energy back home which I miss here. My festivals don't mean much to the people in Singapore. In Bangladesh, if I go out during those festivals, I see everyone celebrating. Everyone is having a holiday; everyone is wearing new clothes, eating nice food, taking part in rituals, all things associated with whatever festivals are meant to be. I get the same vibes from everyone. Here, where I am working or living with migrant workers from different nationalities, they have no attachment for my festivals. Those days of festivities only bring past memories of home. I feel lonely then.

When I first came to Singapore, I had no friends, so on the day of Eid, I was alone in my room, crying, remembering the times spent with my family back home. I remembered how everyone would be dressed so nicely, the children being joyful, happy with new toys or holding balloons. The next year, my heart was stronger. I adjusted. With time, the alienation increased. But as years passed by, I also made more friends here. Last year, I got together with a few of my Bangladeshi friends in my dormitory and cooked something special for Eid. Then we wore nice Panjabi dress and went out. Within the dormitory, I saw other Bangladeshis sitting in small groups, all nicely dressed, chatting, relaxing, taking selfies. That made me feel good. I felt a little of the festive spirit. But that feeling vanished the moment we stepped out of the dormitory and took the bus. Everyone was a stranger, looking at their phones. No one was wearing any special clothes. No one had that look of happiness. They were not feeling what I was feeling just a moment ago. A sense of emptiness came over me.

* * *

On Food and Religion

Bangladeshi construction worker in Singapore:

When I had just come to Singapore I didn't know anything about cooking. At home it was always my mother who cooked. So every night, I would call my mother while cooking. I told her, 'Mother, I have chicken and I have this spice and I have these vegetables.' Then she would tell me what to do.

Filipino Domestic Worker in Singapore:

After coming to Singapore, I know what foods are healthier. When I buy food in Lucky Plaza[88], I ask if there is a lot of oil. I don't like oily food any more. I can bring this knowledge back home.

Yuli Riswati, forty years, migrant worker from Indonesia to Hong Kong:

I am a Muslim, In Hong Kong, I ate what my employers ate, except for pork. I didn't feel bad handling pork. I knew that this was their way of life and my duty was to cook for them. If I want them to respect my religion, I must respect their way of life too.

Erin Cipta, forty-three years old, former Migrant worker from Indonesia to Taiwan:

As a Muslim living alone in Taiwan, I felt closer to Allah and Mecca. I prayed diligently and fasted throughout Ramadan. My Ah Ma was so scared during Ramadan. She became very concerned and kept telling me 'you have to eat, you have to eat . . . '

Filipino domestic worker in Singapore:

When my Ma'am's family went to Mecca, they sent me to her sister's place in Jeddah for three days[89]. Ma'am's sister asked me to convert to Islam so that they could take me along everywhere. In the salon that my Ma'am frequented, the Filipino workers there advised me to become Muslim for my own good, because then the employers would treat me like family and give me respect. So I decided to become a

---

[88] A mall popular with Filipinos in Singapore
[89] Non-Muslims are not allowed to go to Mecca

Muslim. My God is only one. I was doing this (become a Muslim) only for reasons. Don't think God will be angry.

When I converted, they said 'Mubarak,' threw a party for me, and held prayers for me. Ma'am's sister gifted me a ring. My Baba gave me 500 Riyal. I thought it's nice to be a Muslim, because I got many gifts. But they'd wake me up in the morning to pray! (laughs)

Once I spent five days in Mecca with my Ma'am. I followed them to Kabah . . . They hadn't taught me how to pray. Watching them pray in Arabic, I just mumbled the Christian prayers I knew in Tagalog. When they stopped, I also stopped.

During my first Ramadan as a Muslim, I was always hungry . . . The first day was still okay, but I couldn't take the fast any more the next day . . . I took a lot of food to my room . . . There, I ate and came back. Once, when I was cooking, I was about to eat a banana and forgot to hide . . . suddenly Ma'am's son came asking why I was eating. I just said I had red now[90]! I really couldn't take it . . . I was working . . . I was hungry . . . I couldn't drink water . . . They were sleeping the whole day . . . but I needed to work . . . I couldn't take it without food.

* * *

Living with Colleagues

Durga Balan:

When I first came to Singapore, the company put a few of us workers together in one room. We were all strangers but we were all young people, in the same age group. So we adjusted easily. But for the last six years, I have been staying with five other people, mostly from my hometown. We share one room. Of course, sometimes we have problems. It's just like being in a family. In your family you also have problems. Every year, once or twice, there will be some incident. Mostly this has to do with cleaning dishes, say someone has left a dirty bowl in the sink. Then no one accepts who has put it there. They will say I was not there, I was somewhere else. This is the most common

---

[90] Means she is menstruating; menstruating women need not fast

issue, because sometimes people are lazy. But even in the family we have arguments. But we have to adjust and then someone needs to lead and then settle the problem. If someone just can't take it anymore, he just leaves.

Zheng Xiaoqiong, former domestic migrant worker, writer & editor, China:

In factory dormitories, we followed the law of the jungle. Once I lost my mobile phone when I was showering. I had just left it on my bed. It was worth a few hundred yuan, expensive for those days. A new roommate who had arrived just three days before also went missing, without saying bye. Everyone said that she must have been the thief. All I could do was to be careful next time. I heard so many strange dormitory stories; some girls sneaked their boyfriends into the female dormitory; someone fell from the top of a bunk bed and died; a girl got pregnant and gave birth in the toilet. The hygiene situation wasn't too good; contagious diseases spread fast. Many got infected with 'Hong Kong feet'[91] I was infected too.

Well, life in a factory dormitory is not vastly different from a dormitory in school. It's natural to meet people who steal, have mysophobia, or talk in their dreams. Nowadays, I am in a chat group with my former dormitory roommates. We were all young twenty-somethings back then. Even though we complain about the toughness of our lives twenty years ago, we recall them as beautiful days.

* * *

And Then . . .

Sagar (Bangladesh), thirty-five years old, Construction Worker in Singapore:

I was a very good soccer player. I scored goals in every match. I played competitive matches at the district level. People came to those matches just to watch me play. I didn't care if we won or lost, I just wanted to score goals. One day, while working at a construction

---

[91] Athlete's foot

site in Singapore, an excavator went over my leg one day. My leg was fractured badly. I couldn't play soccer anymore. Finally, I played again last week, after almost ten years. We played against a team of Chinese workers. I scored three goals. But I am scared for my leg. There is still a steel rod inside. I shouldn't play again.

Bangladeshi Interior-Design Worker in Singapore:

I have been at the same company for almost thirteen years. I will go back soon. I heard that my company gives a watch to any employee who stays thirteen years. Once I get the watch, I will leave.

* * *

Acknowledgments

We are extremely thankful to all migrant workers who trusted us to share very personal stories. Writing a book of such scope would have been impossible without their selfless support in providing us their precious time, understanding, and consideration. We are also grateful to all the non-governmental organizations and other institutions for providing the connections as well as other support: Empower Foundation (Thailand), H.O.M.E. (Singapore), North-South Initiative (Malaysia), Jan Sahas (India), Alternative Realities (India), Brilliant Time Bookstore (Taiwan), etc.

We are deeply indebted to Ms Debbie Fordyce for her invaluable assistance and feedback at various stages of the book. We are immensely grateful to the team at Penguin Random House for their incredible support throughout the journey of this book, from conceptualization to its final form. In particular, we would like to thank Nora Nazerene Abu Bakar, Publisher, for her round-the-clock support and very timely interventions; Amberdawn Manaois, editor, for her sharp pen; and Mr Gaurav Shrinagesh for having the confidence in us in developing this work.

Writing a book during the pandemic presented its own unique challenges, given that everyone's lives, including ours, were filled with many ups and downs. On that note, very special thanks from us to our three-year-old daughter, parents, extended families, and friends, for constantly assuring us by providing a sense of normalcy while giving us the strength and confidence to pursue our initiative.

A final note of thanks from us goes to all the healthcare professionals, vaccine researchers, frontline staff, and volunteers in governmental and not-for-profit organizations around the world who have been directly or indirectly involved in managing the COVID-19 pandemic. Your courage, perseverance, and sacrifices are what have given us and everyone in the world strength and hope in continuing with our daily lives.

Yolanda Yu and Shivaji Das
February 2022, Singapore